DECORATIVE PAINTER'S
Pattern Book

DECORATIVE PAINTER'S
Pattern Book

OVER 500 DESIGNS
FOR PAPER, GLASS, WOOD, WALLS & NEEDLEWORK

Mickey Baskett

Sterling Publishing Co., Inc.
New York

Prolific Impressions Production Staff:

Editor in Chief: Mickey Baskett
Copy Editor: Sylvia Carroll
Graphics: Dianne Miller, Karen Turpin
Styling: Kirsten Jones
Photography: Jerry Mucklow
Administration: Jim Baskett

Every effort has been made to insure that the information presented is accurate. Since we have no control over physical conditions, individual skills, or chosen tools and products, the publisher disclaims any liability for injuries, losses, untoward results, or any other damages which may result from the use of the information in this book. Thoroughly read the instructions for all products used to complete the projects in this book, paying particular attention to all cautions and warnings shown for that product to ensure their proper and safe use.

No part of this book may be reproduced for commercial purposes in any form without permission by the copyright holder. The written instructions and design patterns in this book are intended for the personal use of the reader and may be reproduced for that purpose only.

Library of Congress Cataloging-in-Publication Data Available

10 9 8 7 6 5 4 3 2 1

Published by Sterling Publishing Co., Inc.
387 Park Avenue South, New York, N.Y. 10016

© 2003 by Prolific Impressions, Inc.

Produced by Prolific Impressions, Inc.
160 South Candler St., Decatur, GA 30030

Distributed in Canada by Sterling Publishing
c/o Canadian Manda Group, One Atlantic Avenue, Suite 105
Toronto, Ontario, Canada M6K 3E7
Distributed in Great Britain and Europe by Chrysalis Books
64 Brewery Road, London N7 9NT, England
Distributed in Australia by Capricorn Link (Australia) Pty. Ltd.
P.O. Box 704, Windsor, NSW 2756 Australia

Acknowledgements

Many thanks to all the artists who contributed their talent to create these wonderful patterns. I can always count on them to share their art with others. Thank you...
Betty Auth
Gigi Smith Burns
Patty Cox
Karen Embry
Susan Fouts Kline
Cindy Mann
Jan McCraw
Helen Nicholson

Thanks to Plaid Enterprises, Inc. (www.plaidonline.com) for supplying the paints (FolkArt® Acrylic Colors, Gallery Glass Transparent Glass Paint, Stencil Décor Paint) for the painted project examples.

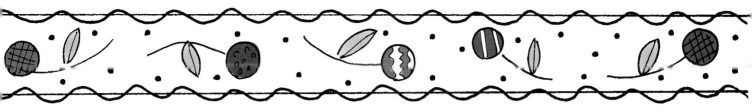

Classic Folk Art Patterns

TABLE OF CONTENTS

How to Use These Patterns 6

Project Ideas

Painting, Decoupage, Ink & Wash, Faux Glass Stain

Paper Crafting, Wood Burning, Needlework

Animal Patterns 24

Birds 47

Flowers 63

Fruits & Vegetables 91

Garden 103

Landscapes 121

Americana 131

Borders & Medallions 141

Garlands 153

Banners & Signs 161

Hearts 169

Angels 175

Autumn 195

Winter 207

Christmas 223

Miscellaneous 245

How to Use The Patterns

There are a number of ways you can use these patterns for your art and craft projects. Following are ideas for a few techniques for which the patterns are easily adapted. The patterns in this book have been colored to help you with color selection. Please feel free to select the colors you desire for your projects.

Transferring the Pattern

For most projects such as painting or needlework, it is easier to use the patterns if you transfer them to your surface.
1. To keep the book intact, trace pattern on tracing paper with a pencil or pen.
2. Position the traced pattern on your surface. Secure it with tape so it will not move. Slip a piece of graphite paper underneath it, shiny side down.
3. With a pencil or stylus, lightly trace the pattern to transfer it.

If you are working on a dark surface you can use white transfer paper and on lighter surfaces use gray or blue paper. If you are working on fabric, you will want to use dressmakers carbon.

Painting on wood with acrylic paint.

Painting with Acrylic Paint on Wood

Use these same instructions for painting on papier mache, canvas-covered items, or vinyl floorcloths. With these surfaces, however, no preparation is needed except for basecoating the surface with paint.

Painting Supplies

Artist Acrylic Paints

These paints that come in plastic bottles are a favorite with decorative painters. There is a tremendously wide range of pre-mixed colors available, as well as the pure colors which can be mixed in the same manner as artist's oil pigments. These paints also include metallic, pearl, and gemstone colors which add glimmer, shine, and luster to your projects. Cleanup is easy with waterbased paints. All you need is soap and water.

These paints can be used on wood, papier mache, paper, terra cotta – most any surface. On some surfaces, it is best if they are used with a medium. Mix them with a textile medium for painting on fabric or with a glass and tile medium when painting on a slick surface like glass, ceramics, or candles.

These are also the acrylic paints to choose when you plan to use a wash technique with a watercolor look.

Indoor/Outdoor Acrylic Enamel Paints (gloss finish)

These easy-to-use acrylic paints are durable, high gloss enamels. This is an excellent choice of paint for glass, ceramics, metal, and indoor/outdoor use.

Some brands are bakable on glass and ceramics for even more durability and weather resistant for outdoor use.

Decorative Painting Brushes

The brushes you use are important tools in achieving a successful painted design, so shop for the best you can afford.

Generally, synthetic brushes are used for painting with acrylics. Synthetic brushes are made from man-made fibers such as nylon or taklon. Often synthetic hairs have been flagged or notched at the ends which allows them to carry large amounts of paint. Synthetic hairs are resistant to breakage and easy to clean.

The size brush you will use at any given time depends on the size area you are painting. Small designs require small brushes, medium designs require medium size brushes, and large designs require large brushes. Trying to paint without the proper size brush is a major mistake.

While flat brushes and liner brushes are the main brushes you will need, there are also other brushes that you will find useful. Descriptions of the various types of brushes follow:

Bright: Brights are rectangular shaped and have shorter hairs than flat brushes. The shorter hairs give the brush more resilience when pushing wet color onto the project surface or when pressing to removing paint from a surface. Because brights can carry a large amount of paint, they can be used for wide strokes as well as chisel edge strokes, sharp corners and details. The shorter hairs allow the painter to achieve textures that aren't possible with other brushes.

Flat: Flat brushes are rectangular shaped with long hairs. The chisel edge can be used to make fine lines and the flat edge can make wide strokes. Because flats have longer hair extending from the ferrule than brights, they can carry a large quantity of paint without having to reload often. Flats can be used for double loading, sideloading, and washing.

Scruffy: Scruffy brushes are wide rectangular brushes with short bristles similar to a bright. Scruffy brushes can be purchased or you can simply use a damaged or worn out brush. They cannot be used for strokes, but they work well for pouncing or stippling, drybrushing, streaking, or dabbling.

Wash/Glaze: A wash/glaze brush is an extremely large flat brush (sized in inches, i.e. 1/2", 3/4", 1", etc.) for applying washes of color and finishes.

Round: Round brushes have a round ferrule and the hairs taper to a fine point at the end. These brushes can be very useful in base painting but are also helpful with strokework. The fine tip works well for painting details and tiny spaces. These are also excellent for using in a watercolor technique with acrylic paints.

Scroller: A scroller is a long-haired round brush used to make fine lines and scrolls. It is helpful for the paint to be thin when using this brush so it flows easily from the brush onto the project surface.

Liner: Liner brushes are round and have shorter hairs than scrollers. These are used to paint small areas. They are often used to paint fine flowing lines and calligraphic strokes.

Filbert: The filbert brush is a flat brush with a tapered tip. Because the tip is tapered it can make very fine chiseled lines and the rounded tip doesn't leave noticeable stop and start marks. It's also helpful for curved strokes, filling in, and blending.

Mop: A mop brush is a round brush with very soft, long hairs. It is primarily used for smoothing, softening, and blending edges.

Stencil: A stencil brush is a round brush with either stiff or soft bristles. The paint is applied either with a pouncing motion or a round circular motion. These brushes need very little paint loaded onto them, and excess paint is dabbed off onto a paper towel before applying to the project surface. They are especially good for stippled areas of painting, as well as for stenciling.

Angular: The angular or angled brush is a flat brush with the hairs cut at an angle. The angled brush paints a fine, chiseled edge and is perfect for painting curved strokes, sharp edges, and blending.

Deerfoot Shader: A deerfoot shader is a round brush with the hairs cut on an angle. It can be used for shading, stippling, and adding texture.

Fan Brush: This is a finishing brush that is traditionally used dry and clean. Lightly bounce the flat side of the brush on wet surfaces for textured effects. Blend the edges between wet glazes to achieve very soft gradations of color.

Rake Brush: The tips of the bristles of this specialty brush are irregular so that, when used with a light touch, only the longer bristles apply the paint. This creates several fine lines to make accenting much faster and easier.

Painting Mediums

Blending Medium: Blending medium will make blending easier. It will keep the paints moist, giving you more time to enhance your artistic expression with shading and highlights. Dampen the area on which you wish to paint with blending medium. As long as the medium stays wet, the paint will blend beautifully.

Floating Medium: This medium simplifies the most difficult painting technique by allowing strokes to be repeated. It is easier to float a color with the paint + floating medium than with the paint + water because you will have more control, and the floating medium won't run as will water. Simply load brush with Floating Medium, blot on a paper towel, then load with paint. Floating medium does not contain extenders, so it will not lengthen the drying time of the paint.

Palette

A palette made especially for use with acrylics is best. There are "stay-wet" types of palettes available that will help keep your paints wet and ready for painting.

Preparation Supplies

Sandpaper: Fine sandpaper (#400) is used to sand the surface of wood projects before basecoating. Fine wet/dry sandpaper (#400-#600) is used to sand dry basecoats between applications.

For final sanding, you can smooth the wood grain with a folded piece of brown kraft paper, if desired. This also gives a nice polished finish.

Tack Rag: A tack rag is a sticky cloth that is excellent for removing sanding dust. Tack the surface after every sanding.

Wood Filler: This is a substance similar in consistency to putty. It is used to fill holes in wood. Apply wood filler with a putty knife. Be sure it is thoroughly dry, then sand it to a smooth finish.

Wood Sealer: Some people prefer to seal the wood surface before painting, and others prefer not to. A good sealer is varnish diluted with water or you may use a commercially prepared wood sealer.. Also bear in mind that when you paint the surface with a basecoat, you are in essence sealing the wood.

Stylus: This is a pencil-like tool with rounded metal ends used to transfer a traced design onto a prepared surface. A pencil or a "dead" ballpoint pen (one that no longer writes) may also be used.

Tracing Paper: Tracing paper is used for tracing a design or pattern. Choose a tracing paper that is as transparent as possible for carefully tracing designs. Place the tracing paper over the design or pattern sheet. Secure with stencil tape. With a permanent marking pen or pencil, trace the main lines of the pattern.

Transfer Paper: This is specially coated paper used to transfer a traced design or pattern to the project surface. Choose transfer paper that has a water soluble coating in a color that will be visible on the basecoat color of the project surface.

Finishes

Matte Acrylic Spray: To simply add a protective finish that doesn't change the appearance, spray with a matte acrylic sealer. You can also spray finished paintings with this sealer before antiquing so you can remove antiquing mistakes without harming your painting.

Waterbase Varnish & Lacquer: These varnishes come in both brush-on and spray and are available in matte, satin, and gloss finishes. You want a non-yellowing varnish. There are also waterbase lacquers. After your painting is completely dry, apply two ore more coats of the varnish or lacquer of your choice.

Preparation of Wood

Sanding

Sanding is usually needed to prepare rough wooden surfaces before painting. Sand the surface with fine (#400) sandpaper until it feels smooth, sanding in the direction of the woodgrain.

Tacking

Tacking refers to wiping a surface that has been sanded with a tack cloth to remove any remaining dust. A tack cloth is a piece of cheesecloth that has been treated with a mixture of varnish and linseed oil and is very sticky.

Seal Wood

If painting your wood entirely with an acrylic basecoat, you may not need to seal the wood. Most acrylic paints are self-sealing. The first coat of acrylic basecoat will seal the wood

adequately. If the wood has many knotholes then you may wish to seal with an acrylic wood sealer. If staining your wood, you will not wish to seal it.

Basecoat

A basecoat is the first coat of paint after the wood has been prepared. Apply the paint to the entire surface using a 1" or 2" foam brush or a basecoat brush. Apply paint smoothly and lightly. Allow paint to dry. Sand the surface lightly before applying a second coat for coverage. Allow to dry and apply an additional coat if needed.

Transfer Pattern

Transfer only the outline of the pattern. Then, once the first layer of colors has been painted and is dry, you can repeat this process and transfer all the details of the design.

Painting Terms & Techniques

Brush Loading

Loading a Flat Brush: Dampen the hairs of the brush with water. Blot of excess on a paper towel. Stroke the hairs of the brush through the edge of the paint puddle, applying slight pressure and pulling the color away from the puddle. The pressure causes the bristles to spread out and pull paint into them. Turn the brush over and continue to work paint into both sides of the brush. The paint should fill the brush and almost reach to the metal ferrule. Stroke the brush on the palette to work the paint into the bristles. The paint should be smooth and even in the brush, with no blobs on the edges or the sides.

Loading a Round Brush: The liner and the round brush are loaded in the same manner. Dampen the hairs of the brush with water or floating medium. Blot off excess on a paper towel. Pull the hairs through the edge of the puddle. Stroke repeatedly, applying pressure to flatten out the bristles. This will pull paint into the bristles. Continue stroking until the paint fills the brush almost up to the ferrule, but avoid getting paint into the ferrule. Do not be afraid to load brush with plenty of paint.

Sideloading: Sideloading is used for shading and highlighting.
1. Dress a flat brush with extender, floating medium, or water. Blot off excess.
2. Touch one corner of the brush in paint. Lift brush. Blend on palette, pulling brush toward you. The color will drift softly about three-fourths of the way across the brush, fading into nothing on the opposite side.

Double Loading: Double loading puts two colors on the brush that blend to make a third color at the center of the brush.
1. Dip flat brush in floating medium. Blot off excess on paper towel until the bristles lose their shine.
2. Touch one corner of brush in one paint color. Touch opposite corner of brush in another paint color. Stroke brush to blend colors at center of brush. Colors should remain unblended on edges.

Brush Techniques

Dirty Brush: This refers to a brush that contains wet color left from your last application. Wipe the brush gently, pick up the next color, and begin painting. There will be a hint of the previous color along with the new color.

Drybrush: This technique is usually used to add a hint of color such as blush to apples, frost to plums, rouge to cheeks, and similar situations. Let your painting dry. Do not pick up painting medium in your brush. Use a scruffy round brush or a stencil brush or even a flat brush. Dip brush into paint, then wipe brush on paper towel until almost all the color is gone. You will be surprised how much color remains. Apply to painting surface with quick crosshatch strokes.

Blending: This is the removal of lines between colors or values. It also merges two or more colors together to create dimension, contrast, shadows, and highlights. After the first blending, which is called "rough blending," you can still see the brush strokes but the lines are disappearing. "Final blending" uses slightly longer strokes and a lighter touch. The brush strokes are no longer visible and the transition lines are gone.

When blending, you can wet the surface with blending medium, enabling the acrylic paints to stay wet and blend longer. Apply the blending medium directly to the surface in the area of the design you are going to paint, then apply the paints to be blended on top of the medium. You must work more quickly when blending on a sealed surface (painted surface) because the paint will dry faster. Using blending medium will help keep the surface wet longer for longer blending time.

Floating: Floating is a method of shading and highlighting. Floating medium is especially designed for floating and it's easier to use than water. Let the basecoat dry before floating color.

To float color, first dip your brush into floating medium. Pat brush on the palette until you see the medium disperse across the fibers. Sideload the brush by pulling down on one corner of the brush over and over until there is an even gradation of color in the brush. Or, stroke on palette, then turn brush over and stroke to blend on the other side. There will be a graduated shading from dark to medium to the light in the brush. To shade, apply the color to the area to be shaded, keeping the dark value in the area to be shaded. To highlight, apply the color to the area to be highlighted, keeping the light value in the area to be highlighted.

Highlight: The lightest tone of a painting. Highlights are warmer. Essentially it is a reflection of the light source and is on the part of the object closest to the light source.

Shading: This refers to the way areas of shadow are represented in a painting. Shadows are cooler and darker.

Pouncing: Use the corner of an old flat brush to add irregular dots of color to your project by bouncing the bristles with paint up and down in an area. Pouncing can also be accomplished with a stencil brush, deerfoot brush, scruffy brush, or sponge.

Linework: This refers to fine-line painting such as for tendrils or scrolls or fine-line details. The paint in your liner brush should be diluted with water to the consistency of ink. As you move the brush, keep it on the tip, exerting hardly any pressure. Pull the brush along, keeping it perpendicular. The brush will follow and paint a fine line. Don't "move" the brush, just let it glide along the surface following your hand. You can use your little finger to balance your hand so that you can move the brush along smoothly.

Wash: To achieve a wash, mix your paint with water (about 25% to 75% ratio). Try to keep your color transparent. If it's necessary to re-apply your wash to achieve more intensity, make sure the first coat has dried.

Spattering: Dip a toothbrush into water and tap on a paper towel to remove excess moisture. Tap the bristles into the paint and run your finger over the edge of the toothbrush allowing paint to spatter the surface of your project. Be careful not to add too much water as the paint will become runny and drip. It's always a good idea to practice on paper before you do this on an object. This is also referred to as "flyspecking" or "speckling".

Finishing

When painting has completely dried, finish with two or more layers of a finish. For a light spray-on protective coating, spray with matte acrylic sealer. For a more substantial finish, coat with several layers of a water base varnish or lacquer. Let each coat dry before adding a subsequent coat. ❏

Painting With Acrylics on Paper

When painting with acrylic paint on paper, the most attractive look is to apply a wash of paint rather than a solid color. This ensures that the paint won't bleed through the paper and that it won't warp the paper. The addition of a pen and ink outline to your design will give your project a finished look.

While this technique is generally done on paper, it can also be used on wood items, papier mache, and even canvas.

Supplies

Artist Acrylic Paint

See complete description in "Painting With Acrylic Paint on Wood."

Decorative Painting Brushes

See complete description in "Painting With Acrylic Paint on Wood."

Matte Acrylic Spray

See complete description in "Painting With Acrylic Paint on Wood."

Paper Item

Watercolor paper (300 lb.) is great to use for framed pieces, greeting cards, or other decorative pieces. Ready-made paper items such as notecards, blank greeting card, place cards, and gift tags are also wonderful surfaces for painting with acrylics.

Pens

Technical pens, available in most craft and art supply stores, are used for the inking. Ink colors generally used are black and brown, but other colors are available. Sizes .005 and .01 should get you started. Any fine-line permanent ink pens can be used.

Preparation

No preparation to the surface is needed other than to place it on a firm surface. Transfer patterns to paper very lightly, remembering that your paints for use on paper will be transparent and heavy lines might show through. (Using a water soluble transfer paper can avoid patterns lines showing through your painting.)

Fill two containers with clean water. One is for rinsing your brush and the other for use on the palette. You must have one container of clean water at all times for making "washes" of paint. You need only minute amounts of paint pigment in washes.

A Wash Technique

To make a wash, simply drop some clean water from your brush onto the palette next to the color being used. Pull out some paint with the tip of the brush and mix with the water. Rinse out the brush and blot it on a paper towel. Now pick up the "wash" of color on your brush. Also use this method when thinned paint is specified.

If you need to **dampen** an area, pick up clean water with the brush and blot on a clean paper towel. "Paint" the designated area with clean water. After touching down a color wash on a damp area, allow it to spread of its own accord.

To **dab** or **touch,** pick up a wash of the color indicated and touch the tip of the brush to a damp area. Allow the color to spread.

Leave white areas when applying the first wash throughout the design; do not attempt to fill in the whole area with color. If you leave some white unpainted areas, it will greatly enhance the natural effect. The white areas will look like highlights.

Shadow areas are generally underneath or behind and between petals and leaves.

To **soften** edges, apply a wash of color. Rinse the brush quickly and blot on a paper towel. Pat the color gently. This will soften the color's edge. Work quickly when softening.

Streaking adds a textural quality to your painting. This is done with a minimal amount of color wash and the very tip of your brush. Barely make contact with the surface of the paper as you follow the pattern lines.

Inking the Design

There are two approaches to the pen and ink with wash technique. One approach is to do the inking first, retracing the pattern lines with ink. The other approach is to paint with washes first, let dry, then add your inked accents. Whichever approach you use, the first stage (either paint or ink) should be completely dry, then sprayed with matte acrylic spray before proceeding to the next stage. For more description of the wash painting technique (done either before or after inking), see "Painting With Acrylics on Paper."

1. Place a folded clean paper towel under your inking hand to prevent any oil from your skin from getting on the paper (or other painting surface). It also helps keep your paper clean.
2. Follow the traced design if inking before painting, or add the inked detail you desire if inking after painting. If you have a "shaky hand," don't worry. Mother Nature rarely produces a flower petal or leaf with a perfect architectural edge. Go with it. A few more waves or ripples will only enhance the drawing.

Finishing

Whichever method you used, spray your completely dry project with matte acrylic spray. If a paper project, one or two coats of this protective finish is sufficient. If a wood project, you may wish to finish further with water-base varnish. ❏

Painting With Acrylics on Fabric

Supplies

Artist Acrylic Paints

See complete description in "Painting With Acrylic Paint on Wood."

Decorative Painting Brushes

It is best to use nylon fiber brushes. Brushes with the slightly stiffer hair will hold the paint for a longer stroke. There also are brushes that are labeled as fabric-painting brushes, designed especially for painting on fabric. These facilitate the scrubbing motion often used when painting on fabric.
See complete description in "Painting With Acrylic Paint on Wood."

Textile Medium

To make craft acrylic paints bond with the fibers of fabric, use a textile medium. You can either mix the medium with the paint, following directions on the bottle, or paint the fabric with medium one area at a time before applying paint to that area.

Plastic-covered Cardboard

Cover a piece of heavy cardboard with plastic to create a painting surface. This will not only protect other surfaces from paint that bleeds through the fabric but will provide a firm painting surface.

Iron

The iron is used to heat-set the painting after paints are completely dry. This further bonds the paint to the fibers for permanence.

Preparing Fabric for Painting

Wash and dry your fabric before painting. This removes factory sizing which could interfere with a good bond of paint and fabric fibers. Sizing in fabrics makes the paint stay on the top of the fabric. Prove it to yourself: Drop a few drips of water on a new garment and watch it bead up. If you plan to wash and wear your garment a lot, it's nice to know your paint is absorbed into the fabric, so wash out the sizing before you begin. Also, if the fabric is going to shrink, it's better to find out before you create your masterpiece.

Position the design area of your fabric item on the plastic-covered cardboard and tape in place to secure.

Transfer the pattern to the fabric with tailor's chalk or water-soluble transfer paper.

When painting, mix paints with textile medium or paint the textile medium on the fabric, one area at a time while painting the design.

Painting the Fabric

Place the loaded side of brush down and pull the paint onto the area. You will be able to paint approximately 2" of area with each dip. Do not **dab**, just *stroke*. Re-dip and repeat until area is covered. Remember you want the project to look handpainted, not silk screened. Areas that are lighter blend together when the entire project is complete. Clean brushes in the water container and dry off on a rag between colors. Swish, swish, swish, dry, dip, continue.

Refer to "Painting With Acrylic Paint on Wood" for some basic painting techniques. However, there is a different drag when painting on fabric. When painting on wood or paper, your brush glides. On fabric, you will need to use a more scrubbing motion.

Finishing

Dry: After you have completely painted your garment, allow it to dry for 24 hours. Be sure to pull the fabric away from the cardboard so that it doesn't dry onto the board. When it's dry, remove from the board.

Heat-Set: With a dry iron, press the painted areas using a circular motion for 10 seconds on all the embellished areas. Or use no motion. Hold the iron in place for 10 seconds, then move it to a different part of the painting and repeat until all is heat-set. Use a pressing cloth to protect your painted fabric project. The most frequently asked question is, "Should I iron on the wrong side?" No, when you paint with acrylic paints they are flat to the surface and absorbed, thus nothing is raised or sticky. ❏

Painting With Acrylics on Glass & Ceramics

Supplies

Glass or Ceramic Paints

There are many paints available that are formulated especially for use on glass or ceramics. These paints are opaque, water-based, and can be used like Artist Acrylic Paints – yet they adhere to glass and are permanent on the glass when washed. There are several types available. Some of these paints air-dry with permanency. Some types have to be baked in a home oven at a low-temperature to make them permanent. Be sure to read the manufactures instructions before beginning to make sure you have purchased the type of paint made for use on glass.

Artist Acrylic Paints can be used on glass; however, they need to be used with a painting medium and they are not permanent on glass so should be used only on decorative items that do not need to be washed.

Glass and Tile Medium

Glass and tile medium makes it possible to paint with acrylics on glass, ceramics, tiles, and other slick surfaces that normally do not accept paint – even candles. It gives a "tooth" to slick non-porous surfaces to make painting easier. It increases the durability of paint on these surfaces and provides a matte finish on both non-porous and porous materials. The surface can be hand- washed. Use on items that are for decorative purposes only. It can also be used as a finish coat on top of your completed and dry painted design.

A matte acrylic spray can also provide this type painting surface.

Glass or Ceramic Items to Paint

A variety of glass and ceramic items can be used. Dishes, vases, bottles, jars, canisters, lamps, candle holders and much more are readily available and inexpensive in craft shops, outlet stores, and department stores. You can find them in secondhand stores and garage or rummage sales even more inexpensively. Blank ceramic tiles can be found at home improvement stores.

Glass: These include vases, bottles and jars, canisters, plates, pitchers, glasses, candle holders, and many other items. They may be clear or tinted, shiny or frosted, and even transparent or opaque. Glass comes in many colors.

Glass items may be plain or embossed with designs or borders.

Glazed Ceramics: Ceramic plates, canisters, vases, lamps, mugs, decorator boxes, teapots and more are easily found in a variety of colors. Most are quite inexpensive. These, too, can be plain or have embossed design elements or borders.

Tiles: Painted ceramic tiles are wonderful for decorating a wall, either as a single small accessory or as a larger tiled area. Or use them as trivets. Tiles can also line a tray or border a vanity. They are available in many colors and in a variety of sizes.

Preparation of Surface

1. If there are sticky labels or grease on surface, use adhesive remover to clean off these substances. Then wipe surface thoroughly with rubbing alcohol to ensure adhesion of paint to surface. To remove surface dirt or dust, wash item first in warm sudsy water, then wipe with rubbing alcohol and a paper towel.
2. Position the pattern in place on your project and tape to secure. The surfaces of glass and ceramic items are often curved or irregular, so it is helpful to cut excess tracing paper away from the design.

For very simple designs, you can use the pattern simply as a visual guide as you freehand your design with a grease pencil or fine tip marker or even directly with the paint. Transfer the traced design onto the glass or ceramic piece with transfer paper.

When painting on clear glass, you can simply place the pattern behind the glass (under a plate, inside a vase, etc.) and tape it in place. You can see the pattern through the glass. Simply follow it as you paint.

Another option is to place the pattern behind the glass and trace it onto your painting surface with a grease pencil, a crayon, or a fine tip marker.

Paint the Design

Paint your design as usual. If needed, refer to painting instructions in "Painting With Acrylic Paint on Wood" for general painting terms and techniques. Let dry.

Air Dry or Bake

You may simply let the design air dry.

For even greater durability on glass, you may bake it in your oven as follows:

1. Let your piece dry for 48 hours to be sure that all layers of paint have dried.

2. Place piece in a cool oven.

3. Set oven temperature for 325-degrees F. (165-degrees C.). Glass must heat gradually to avoid breakage, so don't put it in a hot oven; let it heat along with the oven.

4. When oven has reached 325-degrees, bake for 10 minutes. Then turn oven off. Let glass cool completely in oven. ❑

Painting With Acrylic Enamel Paint on Metal, Clay Pots & Concrete

See metal bucket example on page 1

Supplies

Indoor/Outdoor Acrylic Enamel Paints (gloss finish)

These easy-to-use acrylic paints are durable, high gloss enamels. This is an excellent choice of paint for glass, ceramics, metal, and indoor/outdoor use.

Some brands are bakable on glass and ceramics for even more durability and weather resistant for outdoor use.

Decorative Painting Brushes

See complete description in "Paint with Acrylic Paint on Wood."

Pen Point Tip for Fine Lines

This is a handy craft tool. It is a tip that fits on a bottle of paint that turns the paint bottle into a paint *writer*. When you squeeze paint from the bottle through the tip, it comes out in a fine line with which you can write or draw details.

Outdoor varnish or pour-on resin finish

Outdoor sealer is polyurethane based and gives maximum durability for outdoor projects. It brushes on and dries clear. It is available in gloss, satin, or matte finishes. Use these to coat projects for lasting protection.

Pour-on resin comes in two parts – a resin and a hardener. It gives projects a hard, waterproof, professional-looking very glossy finish with depth and luster. Surfaces are easy to clean when this finish is used.

Preparation of Surface

Terra Cotta: Wash your clay flower pot or other item with a solution of one cup vinegar to one quart water. Apply one coat of matte varnish and let dry before you basecoat or paint your design. If a live plant will be used inside a pot, seal pot inside and out with waterbase decoupage finish and do not apply varnish to the inside of pot.

Concrete: Concrete statuary needs no preparation except to be sure it's clean. However, you might want to seal the surface as described for clay pots to reduce the porosity of the surface; paint colors will be brighter if you do. Planters can be prepared the same as clay pots.

Metal: Wash metal with vinegar to remove any oily residue. Basecoat surface is desired.

Paint the Design

Paint your design as usual. If needed, refer to painting instructions in "Painting With Acrylic Paint on Wood" for general painting terms and techniques. Let the paint dry and cure completely before adding a finish.

Finish

When paint is dry, coat with several coats of outdoor varnish or coat with pour-on resin.

Instructions for Using a Resin Finish.

1. Mix the coating. It comes in two parts – the resin and the hardener. Measure exactly one part resin and one part hardener in a disposable container. Mix vigorously with a wooden stick for two minutes until thoroughly blended. Incomplete mixing can result in a soft finish that won't harden properly. Don't be concerned if bubbles form in the mixture; they can be removed after the coating is poured.

2. As soon as the coating is mixed, pour it over the surface of your project. Spread where necessary, using a brush. You will have about ten minutes to work before it starts to set up.

3. After about five minutes. the air bubbles created by mixing will rise to the surface. The bubbles can be removed (de-gassed) easily and effectively by gently blowing on them until they disappear. (The carbon dioxide in your breath breaks up the bubbles.) Avoid inhaling fumes as you de-gas the bubbles.

4. Discard the mixing container, the stir stick, and the brush to clean up. Allow your project to cure for a full 72 hours to a hard and permanent finish. ❏

Painting with Transparent Glass Staining Paint

Supplies

When using this paint you can create a faux stained glass look. It is easy to do with the special water-based paints and leading.

Glass Staining Paint

Glass stain paint is a special transparent waterbase paint that dries to a textured finish, simulating the look of custom stained glass. It can be applied to windows, glass, mirrors, plexiglass, acrylic, and styrene surfaces. Available in a wide range of popular home decor colors, this paint comes in a squeeze bottle with a special applicator tip, so it's easy to apply paint directly from the bottle to surfaces. The amount of paint needed for a projects varies; you'll need about 2 oz. of paint for three-quarters of a square foot.

PLEASE NOTE: Do not apply this type paint to surfaces when temperatures are lower than 45 degrees or above 90 degrees. Extremes in temperature during the application and curing process can cause cracking and distortion.

The paint is NOT recommended for outdoor use; for surfaces in environments that are not temperature-controlled (storm doors, automobiles, and motor homes); or for surfaces that are in frequent contact with water or heavy condensation.

Ready-Made Leading

Available are lead strips with adhesive on the back. These strips are simply placed on the glass along the pattern lines.

Liquid Leading

This squeeze-on "leading" simulates the look of lead strips. Simply squeeze the leading from the bottle tip to outline designs. The waterbase formula is safe to use and cleans up with soap and water when wet.

Flexible Plastic Sheets

There are 8" x 10" sheets of flexible material on which you can create leading lines, or create a whole design to be peeled up and applied to another surface.

Glass Items to Paint

This glass can be used directly on the inside of windows or on plain glass sheets that can be framed and hung in front of a window. Beautiful projects can be created using simple, ordinary glass and acrylic pieces – plates, bowls, canisters, hurricane chimney, panels, and others – found at craft, department, and variety stores. You may also find items in your own attic or basement or at flea markets and garage sales.

Leading and Painting Your Project

How To Make Lead Using Liquid Leading

Cut off end of bottle tip. Hold the inverted bottle like a broom handle in a vertical position. As leading begins to flow, touch the leading (not the bottle tip) where you want the line to begin. Raise the tip slightly above the surface and move along the pattern lines. The cord of leading will drape down onto pattern line. To stop, lower tip to surface.

For the Modular or Horizontal Painting Methods, your design pattern will be visible beneath your project or plastic sheet. Follow the lines of the pattern.

For the Vertical Painting Method, you will have to make lead strips first, allow them to dry, and then apply them to the surface. To make lead strips, place a piece of lined notebook paper under a plastic sheet and follow the lines of the notebook paper. When dry, these pre-cured leading strips will be peeled up and pressed onto your vertical project, following your pattern lines.

Applying Glass Stain Paint

There are three basic methods of creating your glass art project. The Vertical, Modular, Horizontal.

Vertical Method: Liquid Leading can not be applied to a vertical surface. You must use pre-made lead strips – ones you have purchased already made, or ones you have made yourself. Peel up the leading strips and press them onto the glass project, following your pattern, if using one. Strips can be cut to the length you need or pieced together end to end to make them longer. Do not overlap them. Touch up gaps, if needed, by squeezing in small amounts of the liquid leading. Sections are then filled in with glass stain paint. The paint is squeezed from the bottle directly onto the glass. The section is outlined with the paint, then the center area is filled in. The applicator tip is used to move the paint around to fill the area. A toothpick is then used to "comb" the paint back and forth to smooth it and to remove air bubbles. The paint will dry without sagging.

Modular Method: Both the leading and coloring of the design elements are done on a plastic sheet. Apply the liquid leading along the pattern lines. Let leading dry flat for 24 hours before adding the paints into leaded sections. Let paint dry flat. When dry, peel up the design and place on the glass surface you wish to decorate. The designs created this way are self-adhering. No other adhesive is needed. If desired, background paint can be added around modular designs by the Vertical or Horizontal Methods.

Horizontal Method: For flat projects such as plates, photo frames, ornaments, and glass panels, the entire design can be created directly on the project as it lays horizontally. Do the leading first and let it dry flat for 24 hours. Then fill in the areas with color. Let dry flat.

Using the Patterns for Decoupage

Because the patterns are in color, they can actually be photocopied to provide you with decoupage prints. These can be applied to all manner of decorative home accessories.

Supplies

Print

It is best to color photocopy the design in the book so that you can keep your book intact. The design can be sized as needed.

Sponge or Bristle Brush

This is needed to apply the decoupage finish

Waterbase Decoupage Finish

First use the decoupage finish as a glue to adhere your print(s) to your project. Then just brush it on for a build up of finish that "sinks" the print. When brushed on, the finish (milky when wet) dries to a clear resilient finish. Waterbase decoupage finish cleans up easily with soap and water.

High Gloss Finish

If more gloss is desired, a further glaze or varnish can be added for a final finish. This is optional. The decoupage finish IS a finish.

Small Sharp Scissors or Craft Knife

These are to cut out whole prints or cutouts from prints to decoupage.

Prepare Print

Using small sharp scissors such as embroidery or cuticle scissors, trim off excess around the print, then cut out the actual print. Cut out inside areas (if any) before going around the outer edge. It is not necessary to follow every detail of a print.

If using a single print to cover a whole surface, you may cut the edges with a straight edge and a craft knife.

You may wish to tear out some prints and perhaps to singe the edges for a rustic look. Tear in a downward direction so the underside of the print will have a bevel around the edge and adhere to your project better. Try to obtain an uneven or irregular edge. To burn the edges, use a match or a candle flame to light the edges of the print. Just as the paper begins to burn, blow out the flame on the paper (not the match). Continue burning a small area at a time until entire edge has been burned. Remove excess charred paper by scraping edge of paper with the side of scissors, leaving a brown edge on the print.

Glue Print to Surface

Use decoupage finish as a glue. Lightly coat the back of print with the finish, using a sponge brush or a flat brush.

Place print into position on project surface. Dab print all over with a damp paper towel, damp sponge, or your fingertips. Work out all air and excess glue from under the print, working from center toward edges in all directions. Make sure edges have adhered well. Allow the print to set for a few minutes, then clean up around the print with a damp sponge or paper towel. Let dry completely before proceeding.

NOTE: If you have a lot of small delicate design pieces to adhere, it may be easier to brush the decoupage finish onto the surface rather than the backs of the paper pieces. Use a damp paper towel or sponge to press down each print for firm adhesion and to remove excess finish from surface.

Apply Decoupage Finish

Apply decoupage finish to entire project, using a sponge brush or a flat brush. Allow finish to dry approximately 20 minutes until clear and dry. Apply a second coat of finish. Two coats may be sufficient to submerge and protect print; you may apply more, if desired. If you desire a completely smooth satin finish, apply at least six coats of finish, then follow the optional "Final Finish" step.

Final Finish

OPTIONAL: This step will give you the satin smooth look of traditional decoupage.

Wet #400 sandpaper with water and sand finish lightly until flat and smooth. Wipe dry. Polish project with #0000 steel wool. For an even glossier finish, you may dip the steel wool into a liquid paste of linseed oil and pumice. Gently polish surface with this until smooth.

Creating a High Shine finish: If you desire a high gloss finish on your project, wait a week for the decoupage finish to cure, then add a final finish of high gloss varnish, lacquer, or glaze.

Using the Patterns for Needlework

Many of the patterns in this book can be expressed with needlework, using the colors for suggestions as to fabric and thread colors.

Applique: Cut out various elements of the design from fabric scraps. Arrange the pieces like a picture puzzle on fabric backing or a garment and stitch them in place with a satin zigzag stitch around the edges or glue them in place with fabric glue.

Embroidery: Transfer the pattern to the fabric to be embroidered (see "Painting With Acrylics on Fabric" for discussion of transfer methods). Embroider the areas of the design as desired.

Cross Stitch: Transfer the pattern to tracing paper. Enlarge or reduce it to fit the scale of graph paper, and transfer adjusted pattern onto graph paper. Using the original pattern as a visual guide for color placement, graph your stitching pattern onto the graph paper within the transferred pattern outlines.

Using Patterns for Woodburning

Supplies

Woodburning Tool

The solid shaft woodburner is packaged with a wire holder and at least one point. A good starter point is the flow point, which has a rounded end and moves freely over the surface to produce a line. Several point styles are available for specific purposes, and points can be purchased as an assortment that includes the most common ones.

Cautions: Remember that the woodburning point will reach a temperature of 950 to over 1000 degrees Fahrenheit. It is perfectly safe to use as long as certain safety measures are taken, and the rules are followed. Children under 12 should not be allowed to use a woodburner without close adult supervision at all times, and a junior woodburning tool is recommended for them. It only reaches a temperature of between 600 to 750 degrees Fahrenheit.

Workspace Set-Up Supplies

In addition to the woodburning tool and the points, you'll need a few additional items when setting up your work space:

A **4" ceramic tile**, for taping down the wire holder for the woodburner. The tile is heavy enough so it won't move around on the work surface, and it is heatproof.

A **container**, such as a metal lid, a glass dish, or ceramic plate, to place the hot burner points in until they cool. When removed from the hot woodburner, the points retain their heat for a couple of minutes, so they need to be treated with care.

A pair of **needlenose pliers** with plastic or rubber-coated handles, for removing the hot point from the woodburner and replacing it with a different one. After changing a hot point, the pliers retain the heat for a couple of minutes, so it's a good idea to rest the metal part of the pliers on the points container until cool.

A folded **piece of sandpaper**, for cleaning carbon buildup from the hot point.

Aluminum foil or other heat-resistant material, to cover your work surface.

Paints & Stains

Acrylic craft paints, which are available pre-mixed in a huge range of colors and glittering metallics, can be used to color and accent designs. **Stains and glazes**, both water or oil-based, can be used to color the designs. You can buy pre-mixed stains and glazes or mix your own using **neutral glazing medium** (a transparent liquid or gel) and acrylic paint. The medium's long drying time allows you to blot and rub colors for a variety of effects.

Oil Pencils

Oil color pencils are an alternative to coloring the designs. They are constructed of an oil pigment contained in a wax base. The pencils come in a large array of colors and can be layered and blended.

Finishing Supplies

• **Spray-on matte acrylic sealer** is used for sealing the oil pencil coloring. Matte sealer spray can be used as a final sealer on pieces that won't get heavy use.
• **Brush-on acrylic varnish**, available in matte, satin, and gloss sheens, is used to finish pieces that get heavy use and as a sealer to mask areas of designs to protect them from stains or glazes. Apply them with a flat, soft bristle brush or sponge brush.

The Woodburning Technique

Preparing the Woodburner

To set up your woodburner, tape the wire holder that comes with it to a ceramic tile. Then tape the tile to the work surface to secure it. Use needlenose pliers to insert a point into the end of the woodburner shaft. Tighten to secure. Rest the woodburner on the wire holder and plug it in. It will take four or five minutes to heat fully. Whenever the burner is not in use, rest it on the wire holder. Unplug it when you finish the woodburning portion of your design.

Cleaning the Point: While you work with the woodburner, you will probably accumulate debris on the point. Keep a square of medium grit sandpaper handy. Occasionally wipe the point across the sandpaper to clean off the debris. Check the cooled points occasionally and sand them as needed to keep them bright and shiny.

Burning the Wood

To achieve the darkest, deepest burn, hold the woodburner as you would a pen or pencil, and move at about half the speed you would use when writing or drawing. While burning, keep the point moving. If you stop, lift the point from the surface to avoid dark blotches, spots,

and unwanted burns. The darkness of the burn is controlled by the length of time the point is touching the surface, not by pushing the point into the wood.

Most of the time, you will want to maintain a solid, even, flowing line. The best way to achieve this is to hold the burner lightly, turning the wood as you go so that you are pulling the line toward you rather than pushing it away from you. For small skips in the line, re-burn the area with short "chicken scratching" or sketching movements.

Practice on a scrap of wood before starting any projects.

You might practice by first penciling, then burning your name and the date. Write very slowly, letting the point flow across the surface. Lift the surface from the surface when you begin or end a line to avoid making a darker dot.

If you accidentally make a small burning error, you may be able to sand it away with fine grit sandpaper, then erase remaining marks with an ink eraser. Larger errors are permanent, and you will need to find a way to incorporate them into your design.

ANIMALS

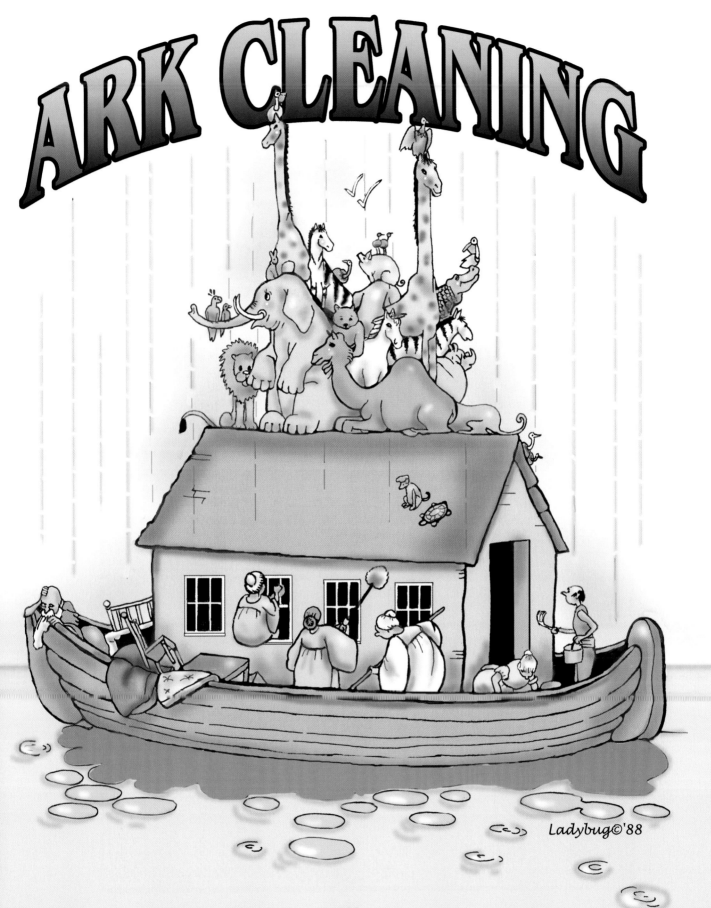

ARK CLEANING

Ladybug©'88

Susan Fouts-Kline

Cindy Mann

Gigi Smith-Burns

28

Susan Fouts-Kline

Ladybug©'86

Betty Auth

Patty Cox

Karen Embry

33

Helen Nicholson

34

Susan Fouts-Kline

Karen Embry

Patty Cox

Susan Fouts-Kline

Cindy Mann

40 Helen Nicholson

Susan Fouts-Kline

Karen Embry

43

44

Susan Fouts-Kline

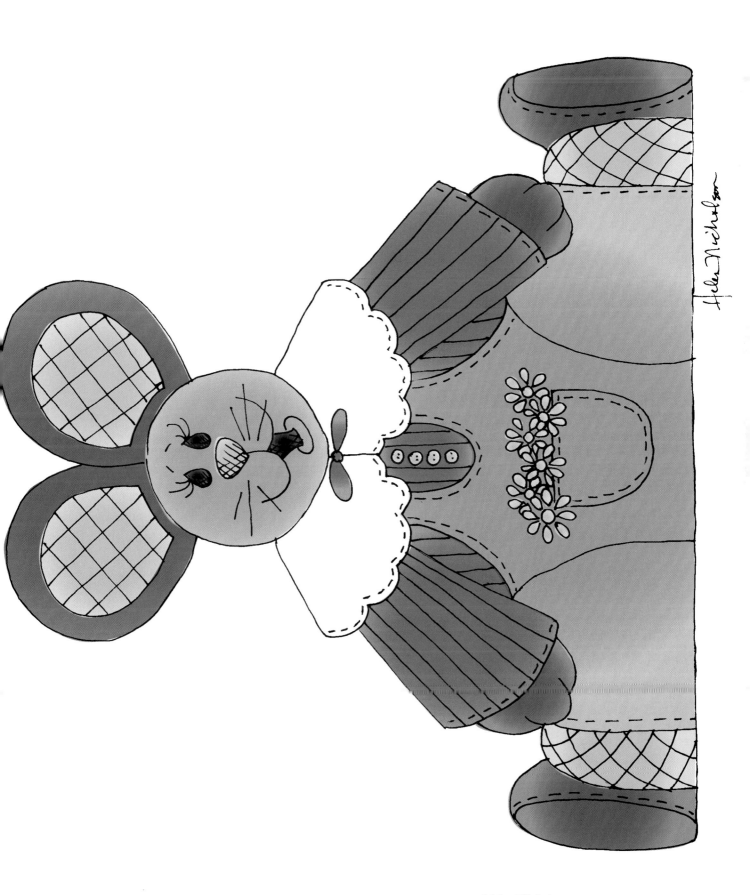

Helen Nicholson

BIRDS

48

Susan Fouts-Kline

Karen Embry

Ladybug

Patty Cox

52

Betty Auth

Gigi Smith-Burns

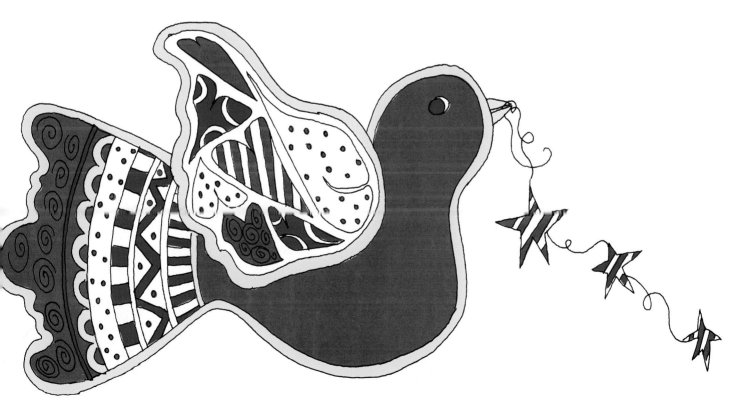

53

Karen Embry

Betty Auth

55   *Susan Fouts-Kline*

56

57

Susan Fouts-Kline

Borders used

Ladybug©'87

58

59

Susan Fouts-Kline

Gigi Smith-Burns

Susan Fouts-Kline

Gigi Smith-Burns

FLOWERS

Gigi Smith-Burns

Gigi Smith-Burns

Susan Fouts-Kline

Helen Nicholson

Karen Embry

Betty Auth

Gigi Smith-Burns

Gigi Smith-Burns

Susan Fouts-Kline

Helen Nicholson

Karen Embry

76   *Betty Auth*

Karen Embry

Gigi Smith-Burns

Gigi Smith-Burns

Susan Fouts-Kline

Helen Nicholson

Karen Embry

83

Gigi Smith-Burns

Gigi Smith-Burns

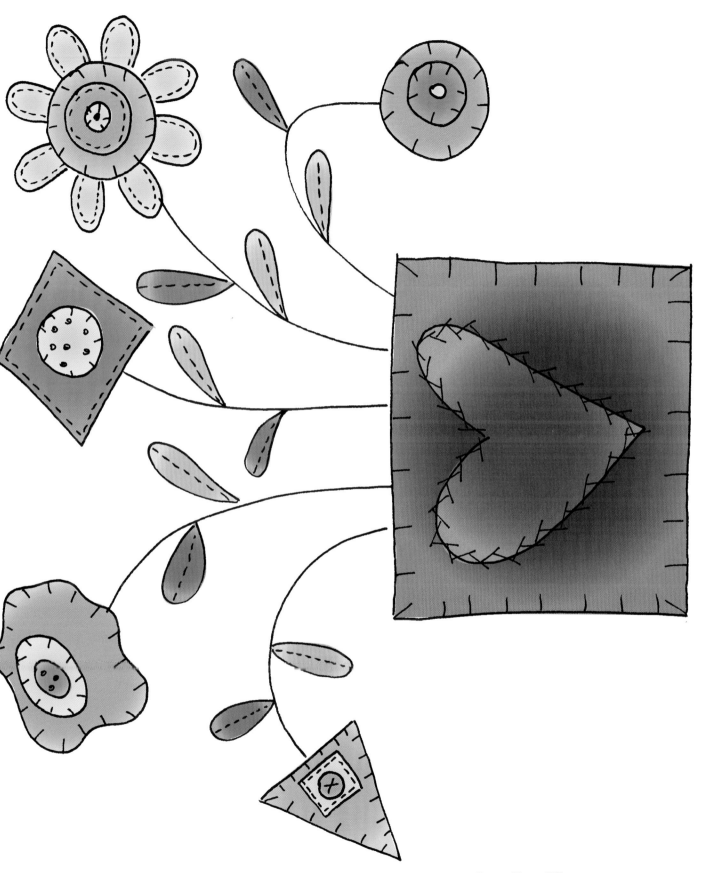

85

Susan Fouts–Kline

Helen Nicholson

Gigi Smith-Burns

Helen Nicholson

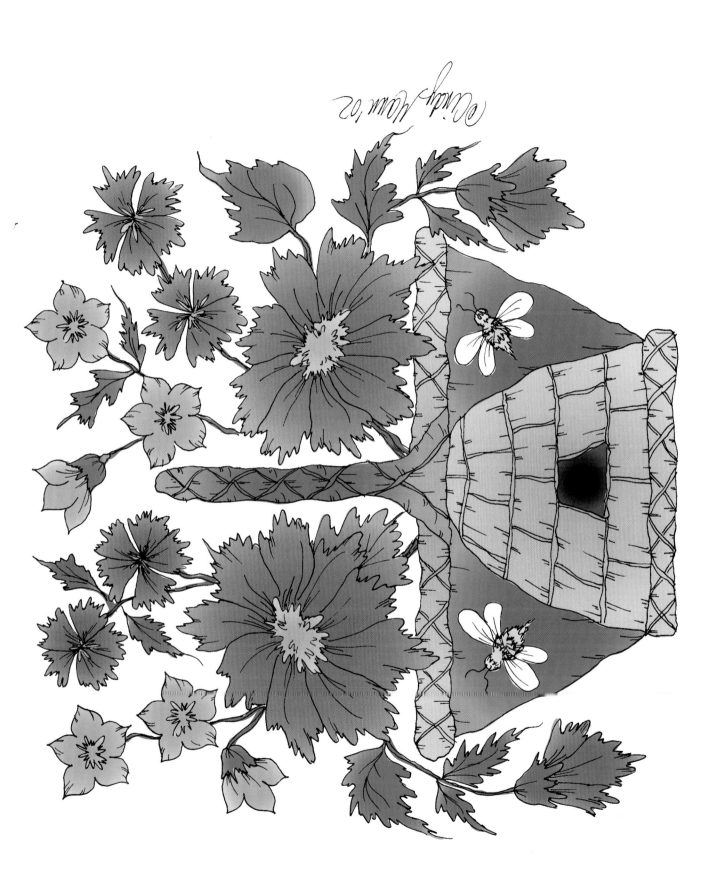

89

Cindy Mann

FRUITS & VEGETABLES

Betty Auth

Susan Fouts-Kline

94

95   *Gigi Smith-Burns*

Susan Fouts-Kline

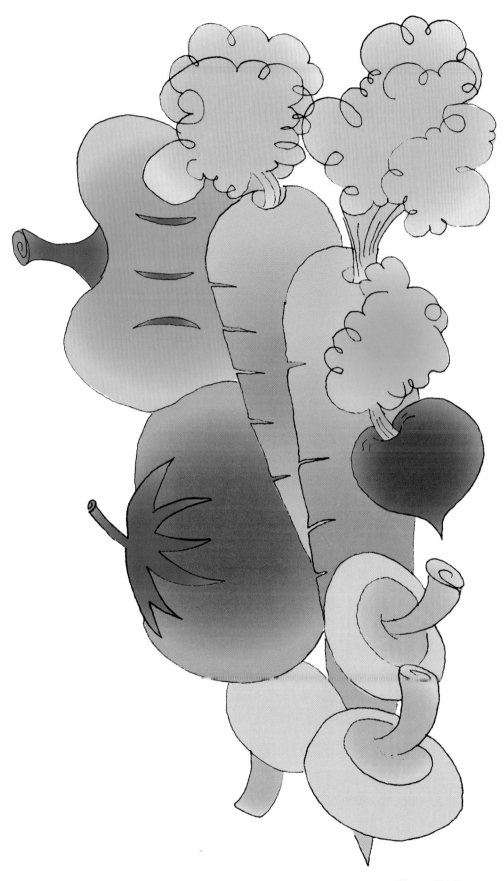

Karen Embry

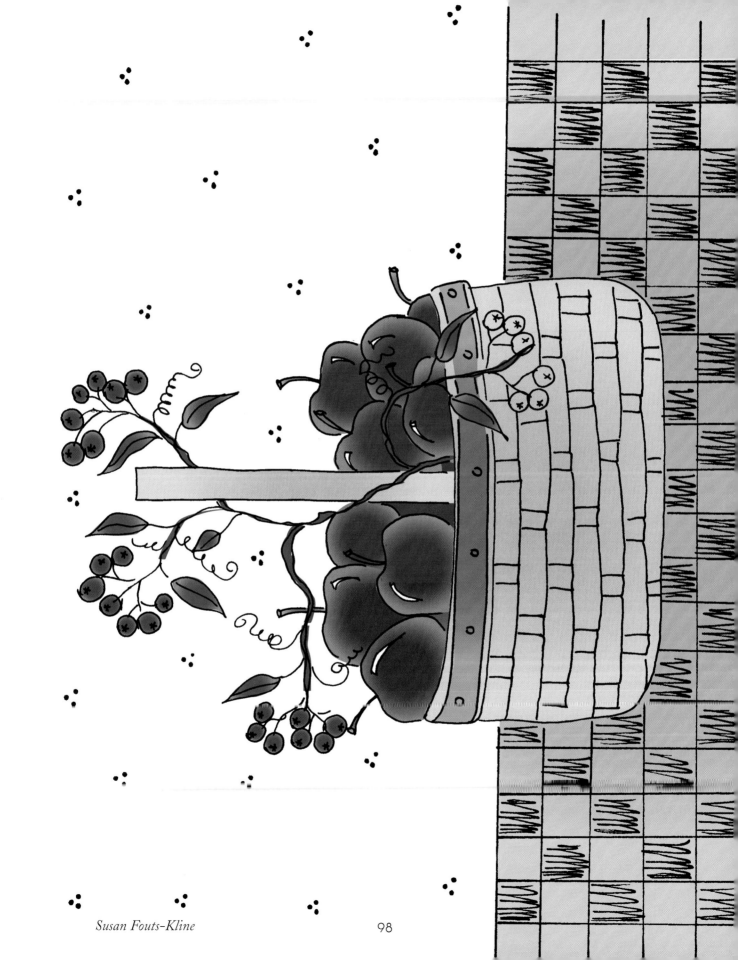

Cindy Mann

Karen Embry

Cindy Mann

GARDEN

Patty Cox

105

Susan Fouts-Kline

106

Susan Fouts-Kline

Karen Embry

Gigi Smith-Burns

111

112

Susan Fouts-Kline

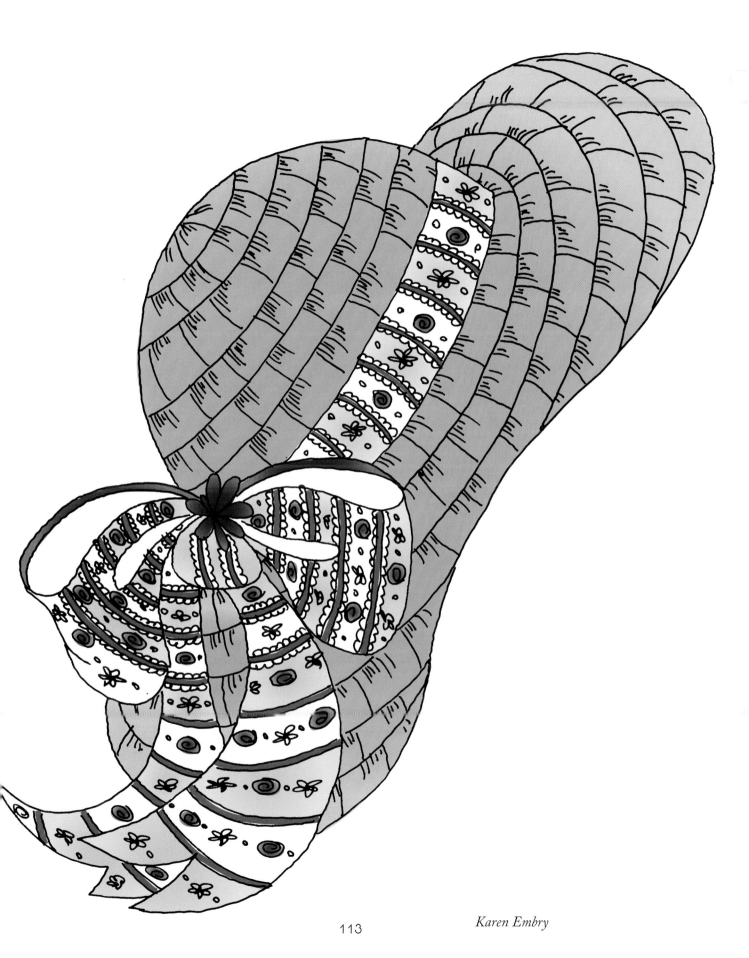

113 *Karen Embry*

Gigi Smith-Burns

115

Gigi Smith-Burns

117

Gigi Smith-Burns

118   *Gigi Smith-Burns*

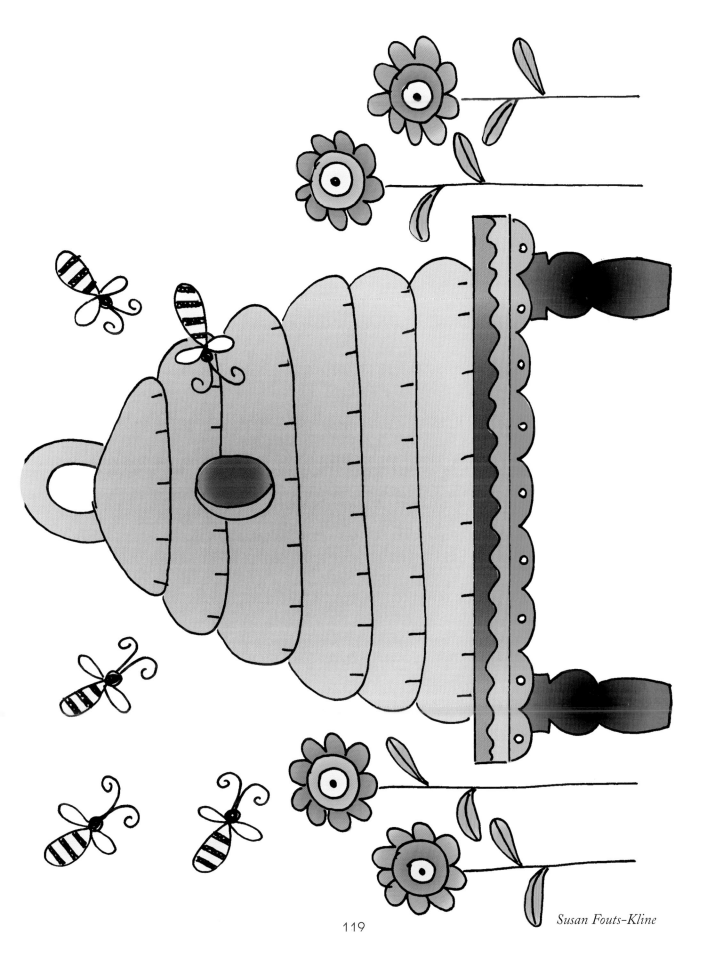

Susan Fouts-Kline

LANDSCAPES

122

Gigi Smith-Burns

123

Susan Fouts-Kline

124

Susan Fouts-Kline

125

Susan Fouts-Kline

Karen Embry

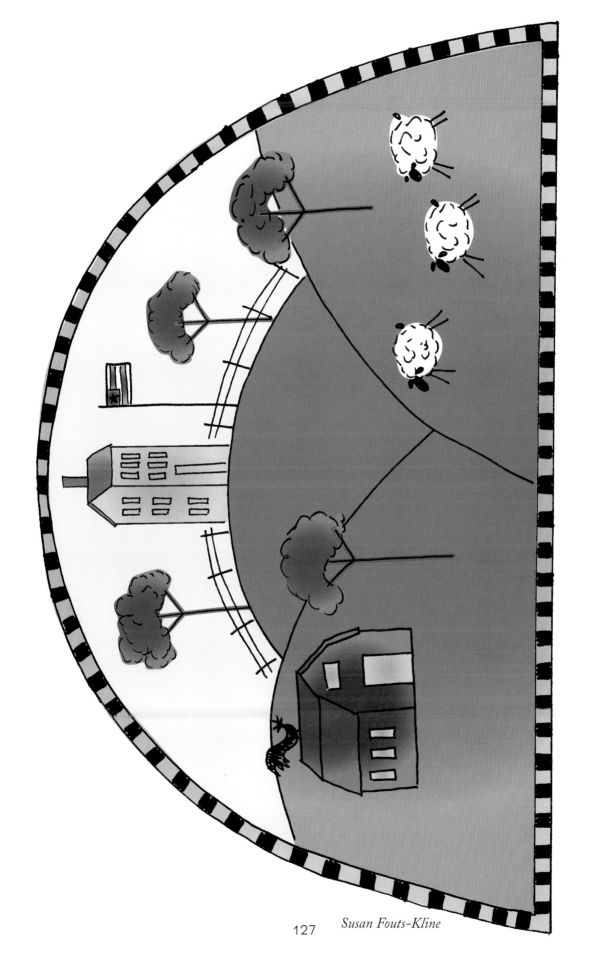

127   *Susan Fouts-Kline*

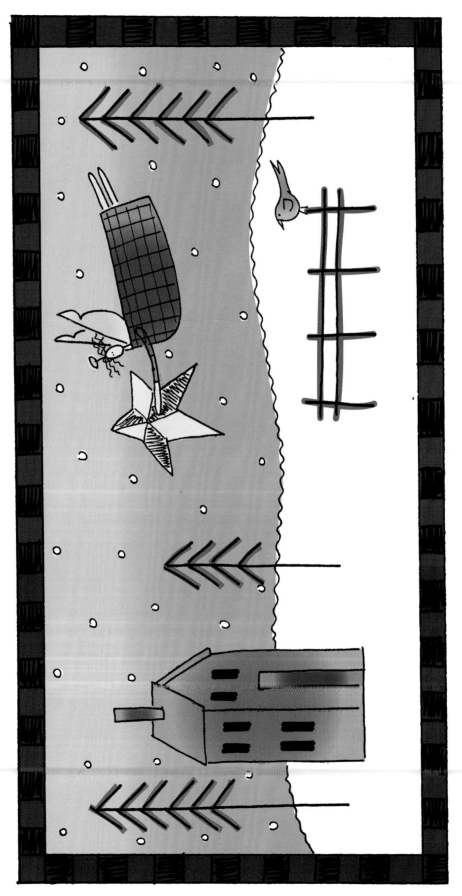

Susan Fouts-Kline

Susan Fouts-Kline

AMERICANA

132

Betty Auth

133

Susan Fouts-Kline

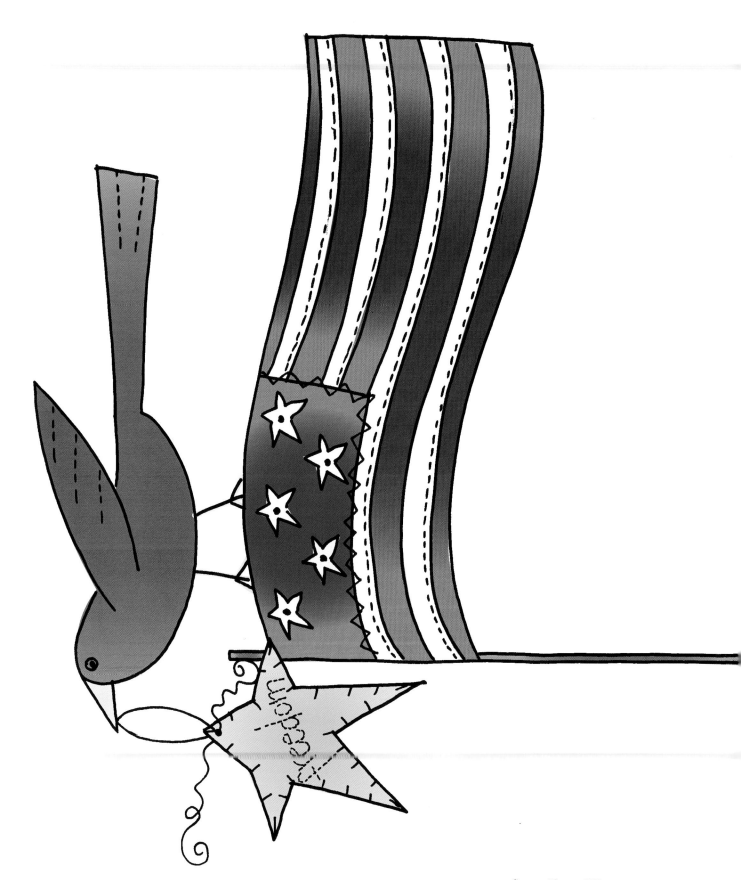

134   *Susan Fouts-Kline*

135

Helen Nicholson

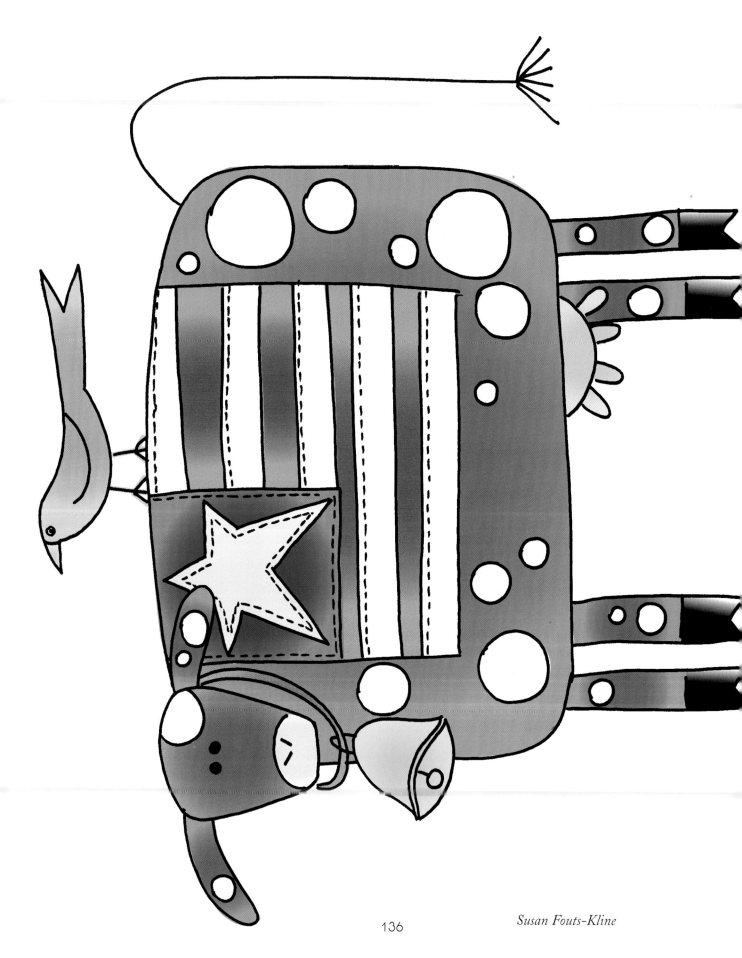

136

Susan Fouts-Kline

137 *Karen Embry*

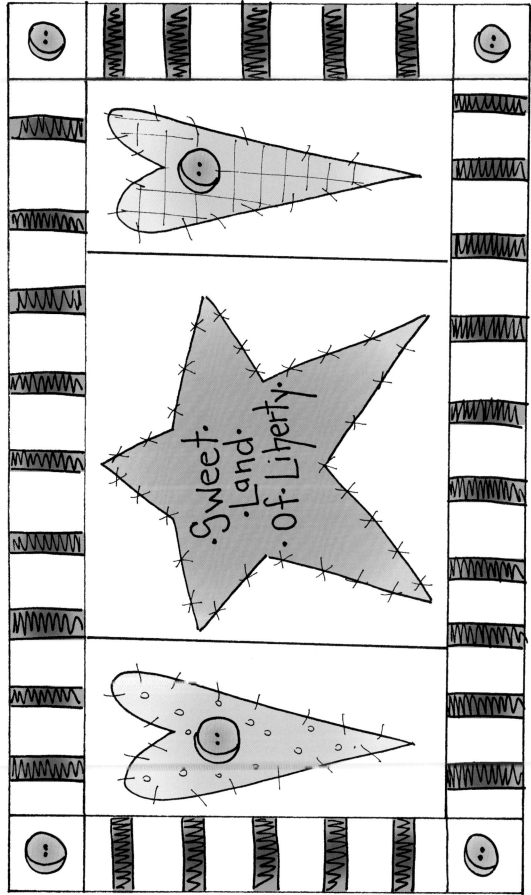

Susan Fouts-Kline

139   *Susan Fouts-Kline*

BORDERS
&
MEDALLIONS

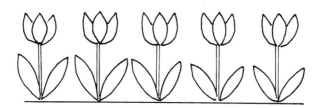

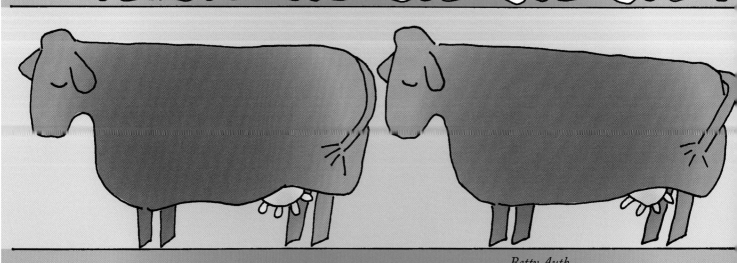

Betty Auth

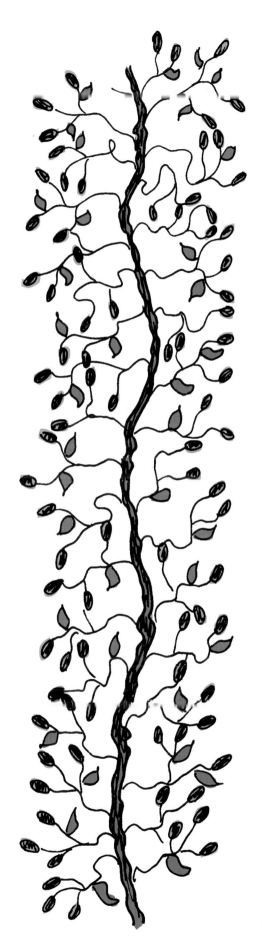

143

Susan Fouts-Kline

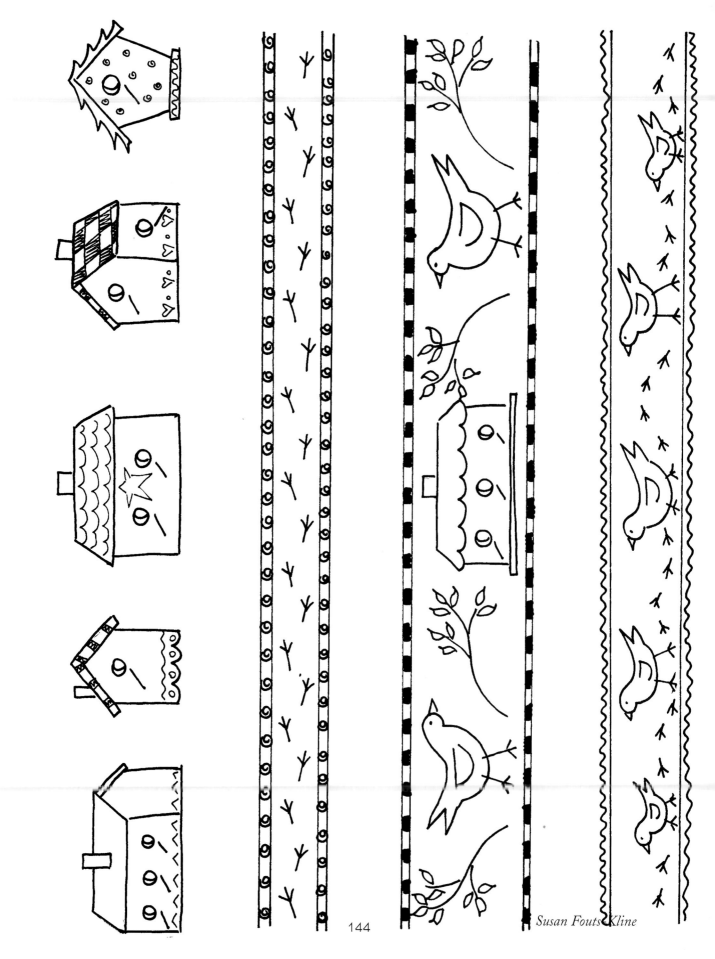

144

Susan Fouts Kline

145

Susan Fouts-Kline

146

Betty Auth

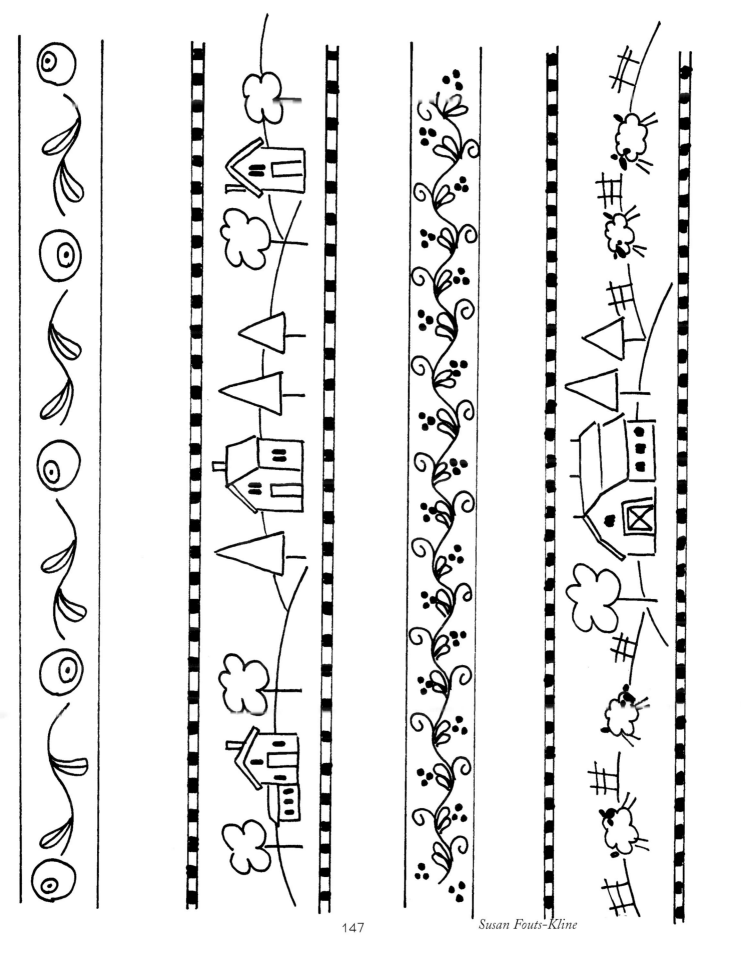

147

Susan Fouts-Kline

148

Betty Auth

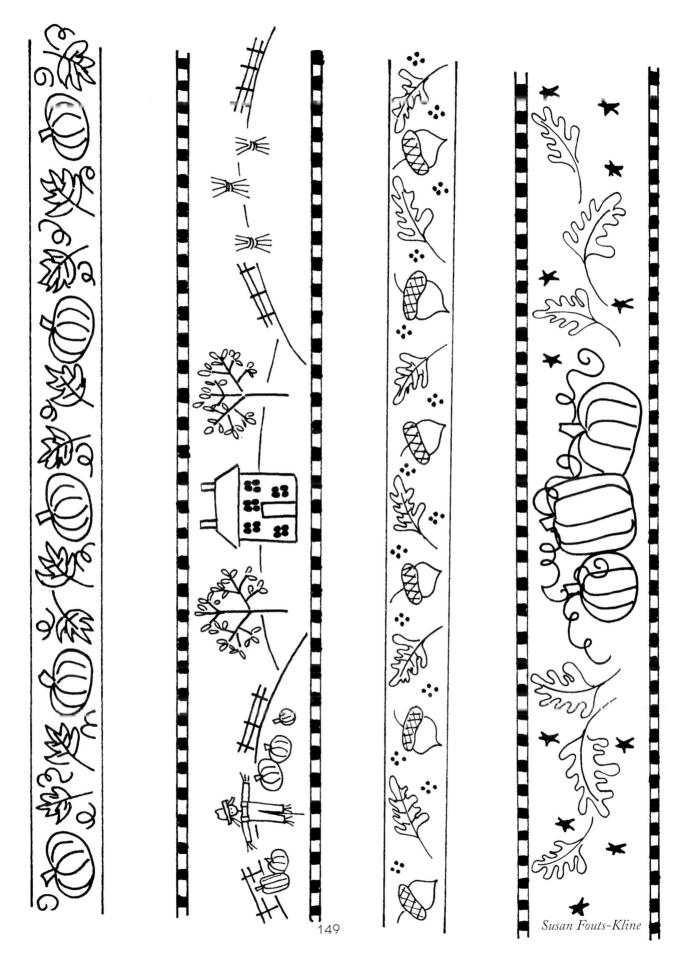

149

Susan Fouts-Kline

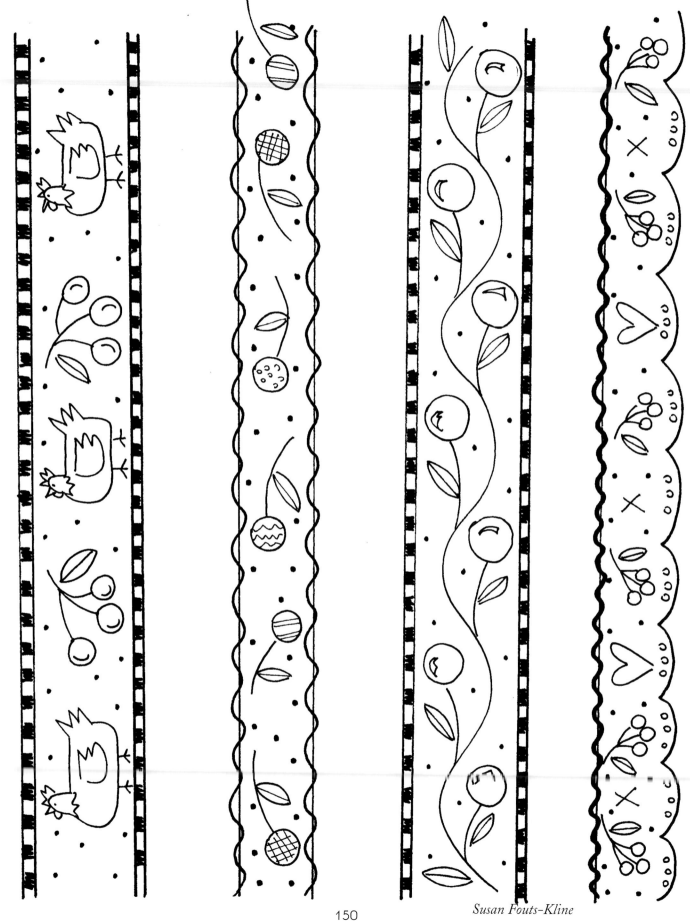

150

Susan Fouts-Kline

151   *Betty Auth*

GARLANDS

154   *Gigi Smith-Burns*

155

Gigi Smith–Burns

Gigi Smith-Burns

Gigi Smith-Burns

158

Helen Nicholson

159

Karen Embry

BANNERS
&
SIGNS

Garden Greetings

Helen Nicholson

YOU ARE MY SUNSHINE

Gigi Smith-Burns

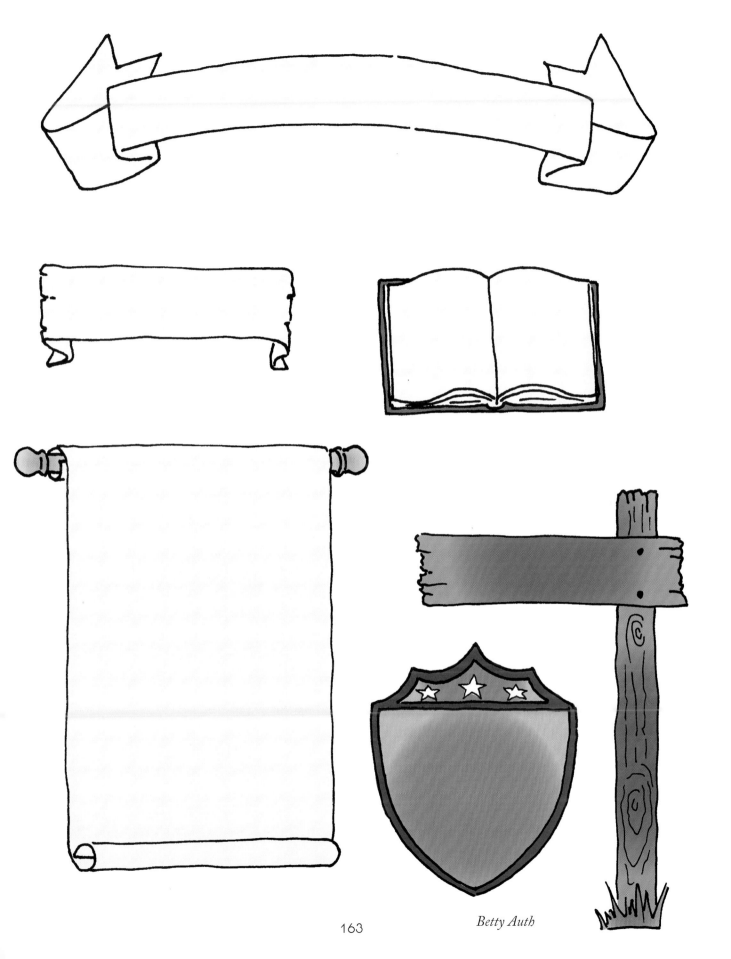

Betty Auth

164

Helen Nicholson

Family and Friends Forever

Susan Fouts-Kline

HEARTS

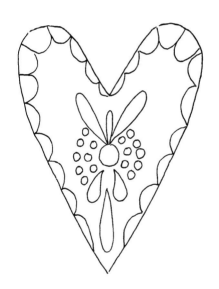

Karen Embry

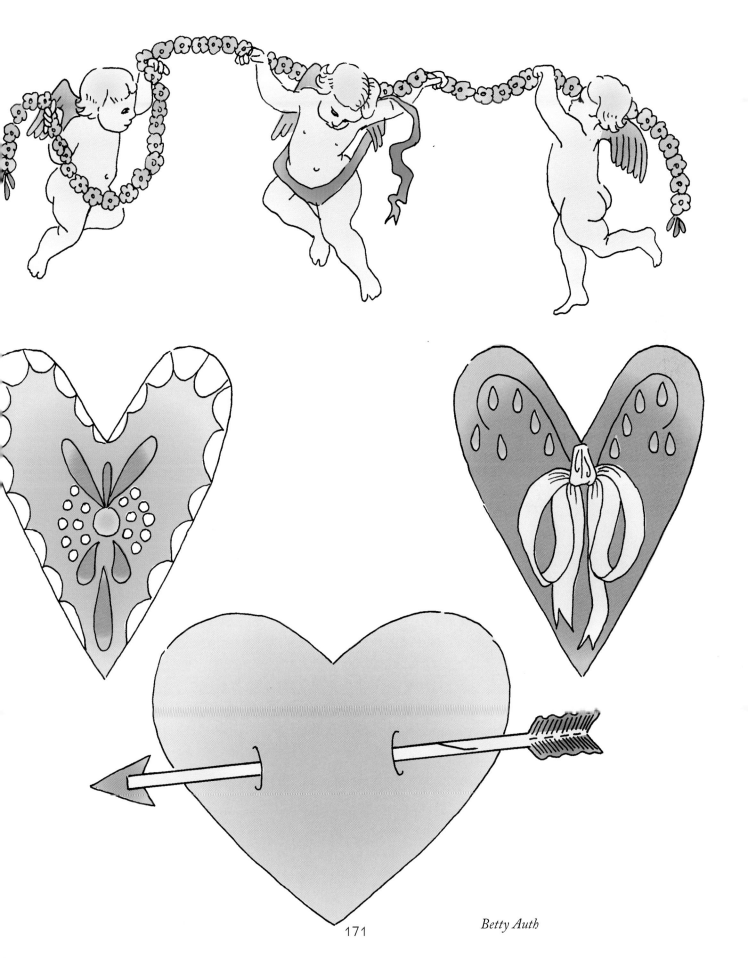

171

Betty Auth

172

Gigi Smith-Burns

Susan Fouts-Kline

ANGELS

176

Gigi Smith-Burns

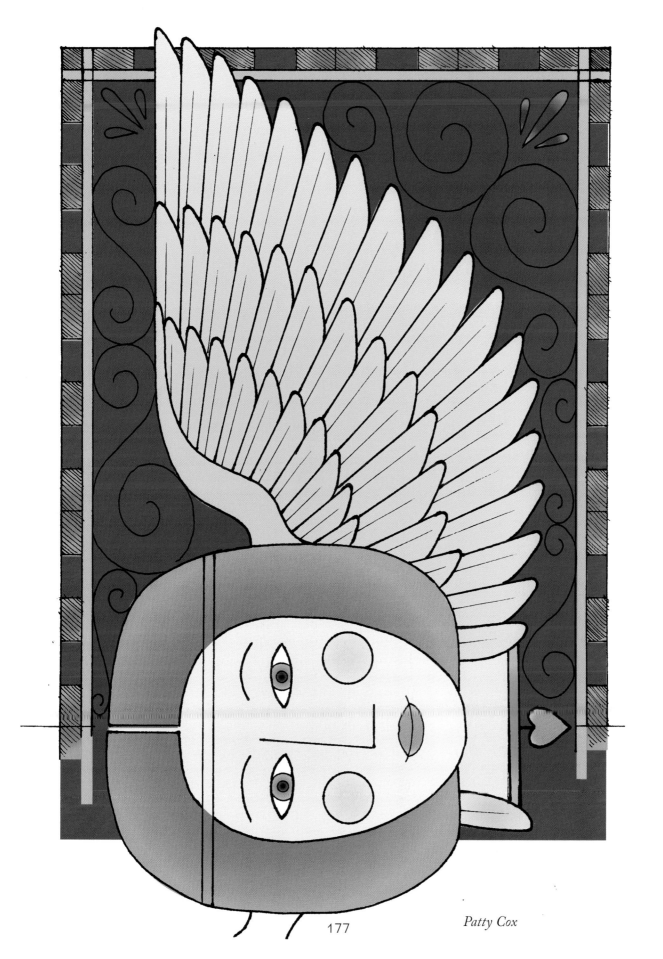

177

Patty Cox

Susan Fouts-Kline

179

Gigi Smith-Burns

Susan Fouts-Kline

Cindy Mann

Susan Fouts-Kline

Helen Nicholson

184

Susan Fouts-Kline

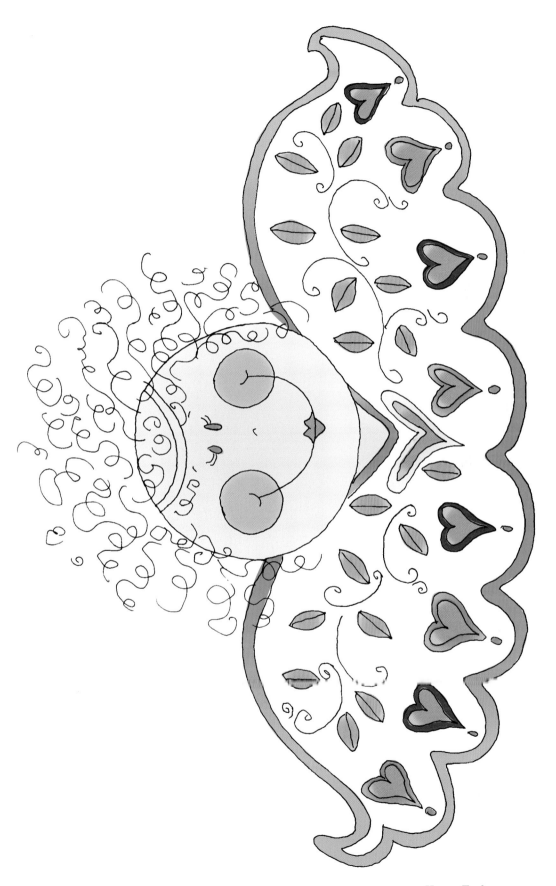

Karen Embry

Cindy Mann

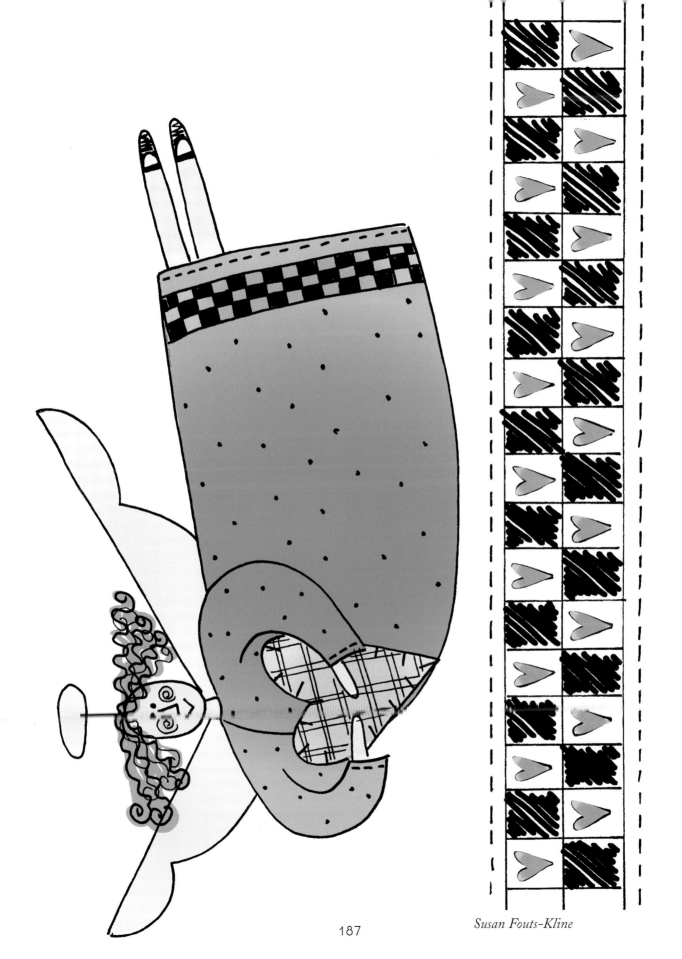

Susan Fouts-Kline

188

Karen Embry

189   *Helen Nicholson*

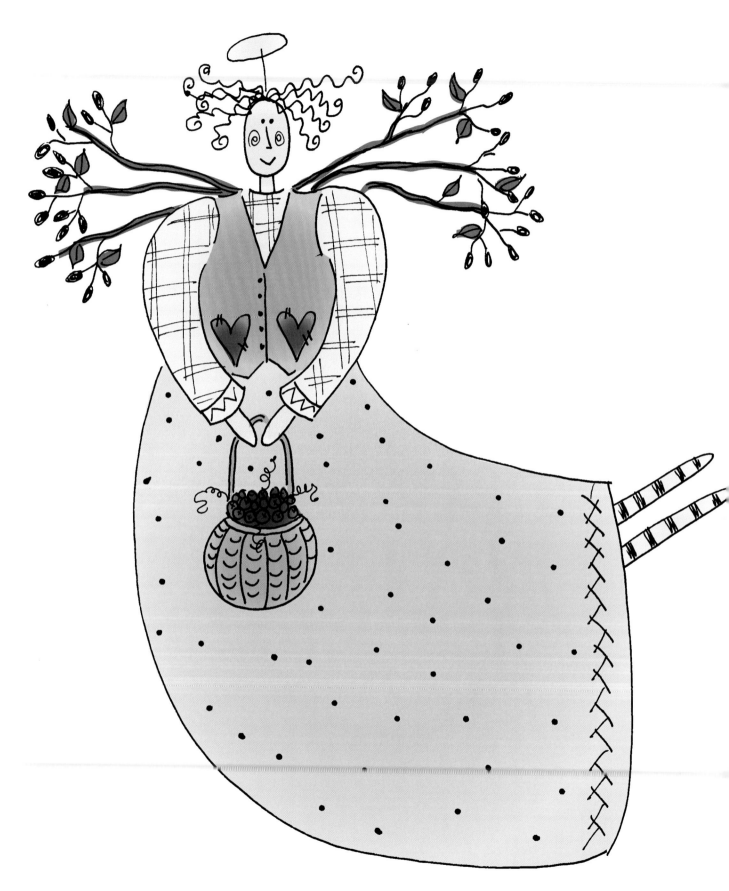

Susan Fouts-Kline

191   *Helen Nicholson*

192

Susan Fouts-Kline

193   Cindy Mann

AUTUMN

Boo
to
You!

Susan Fouts-Kline

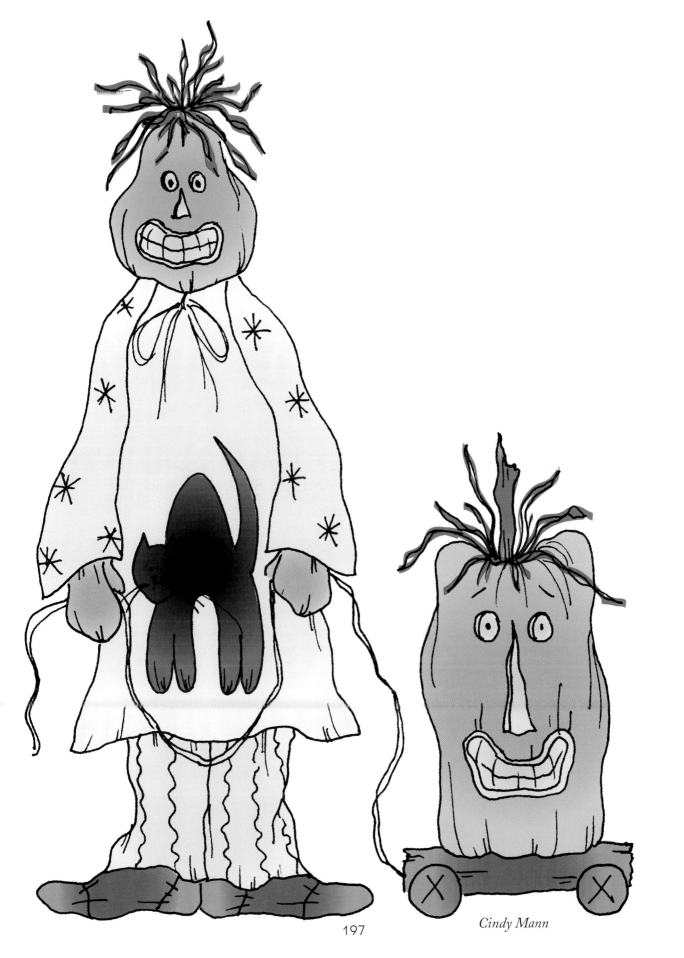

197

Cindy Mann

Susan Fouts-Kline

Cindy Mann

Susan Fouts-Kline

Susan Fouts-Kline

Karen Embry

204

Cindy Mann

Cindy Mann

WINTER

208   *Helen Nicholson*

Susan Fouts-Kline

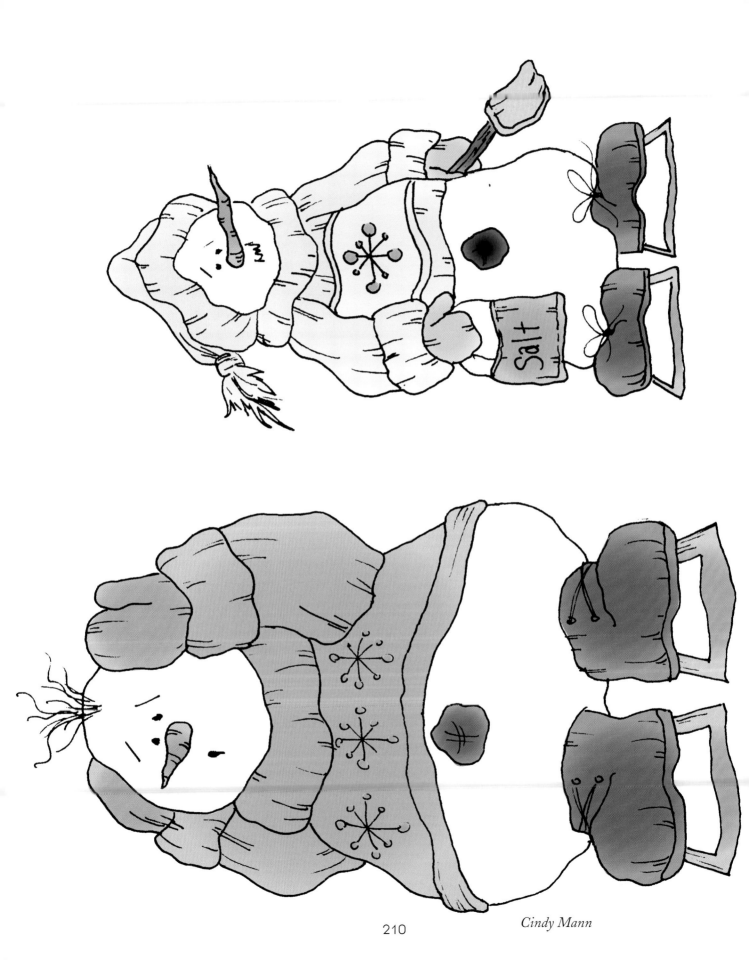

210

Cindy Mann

211

Cindy Mann

213

Susan Fouts-Kline

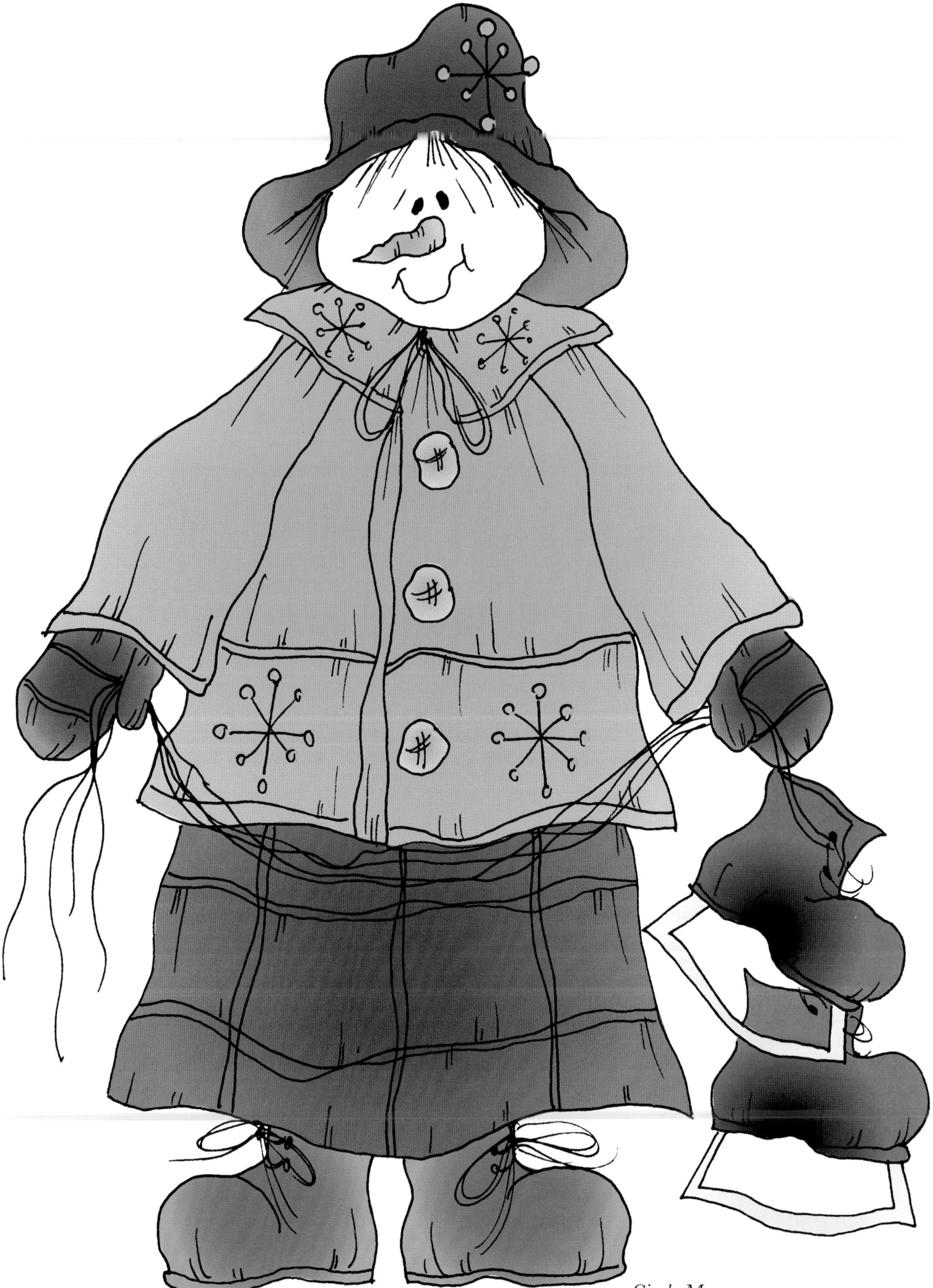

Cindy Mann

Susan Fouts-Kline

Cindy Mann

Karen Embry

Susan Fouts-Kline

Cindy Mann

Cindy Mann

221

Helen Nicholson

222

Susan Fouts-Kline

CHRISTMAS

"Reach for the Stars"

Helen Nicholson

225

Cindy Mann

226

Susan Fouts-Kline

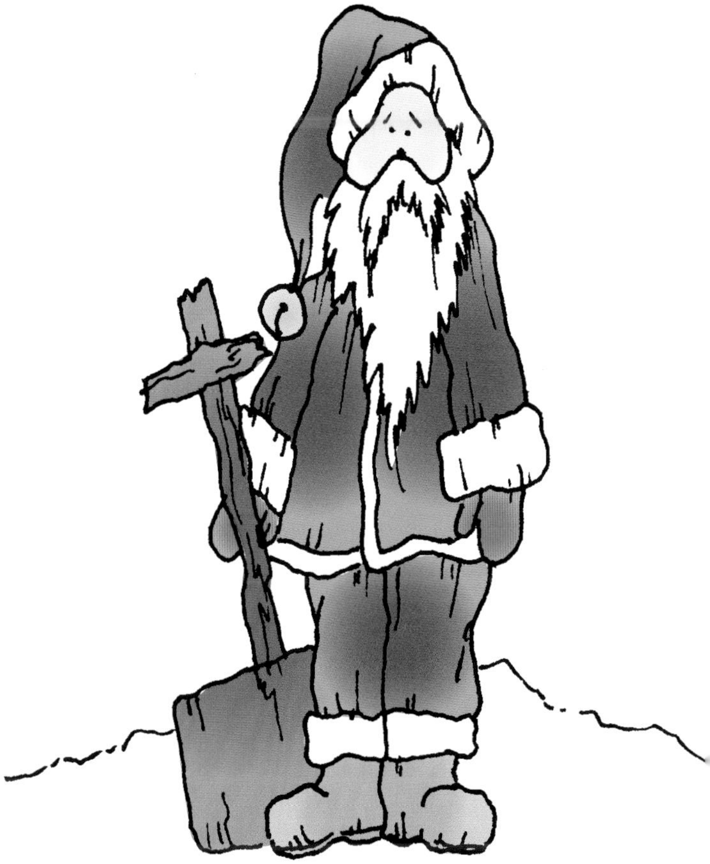

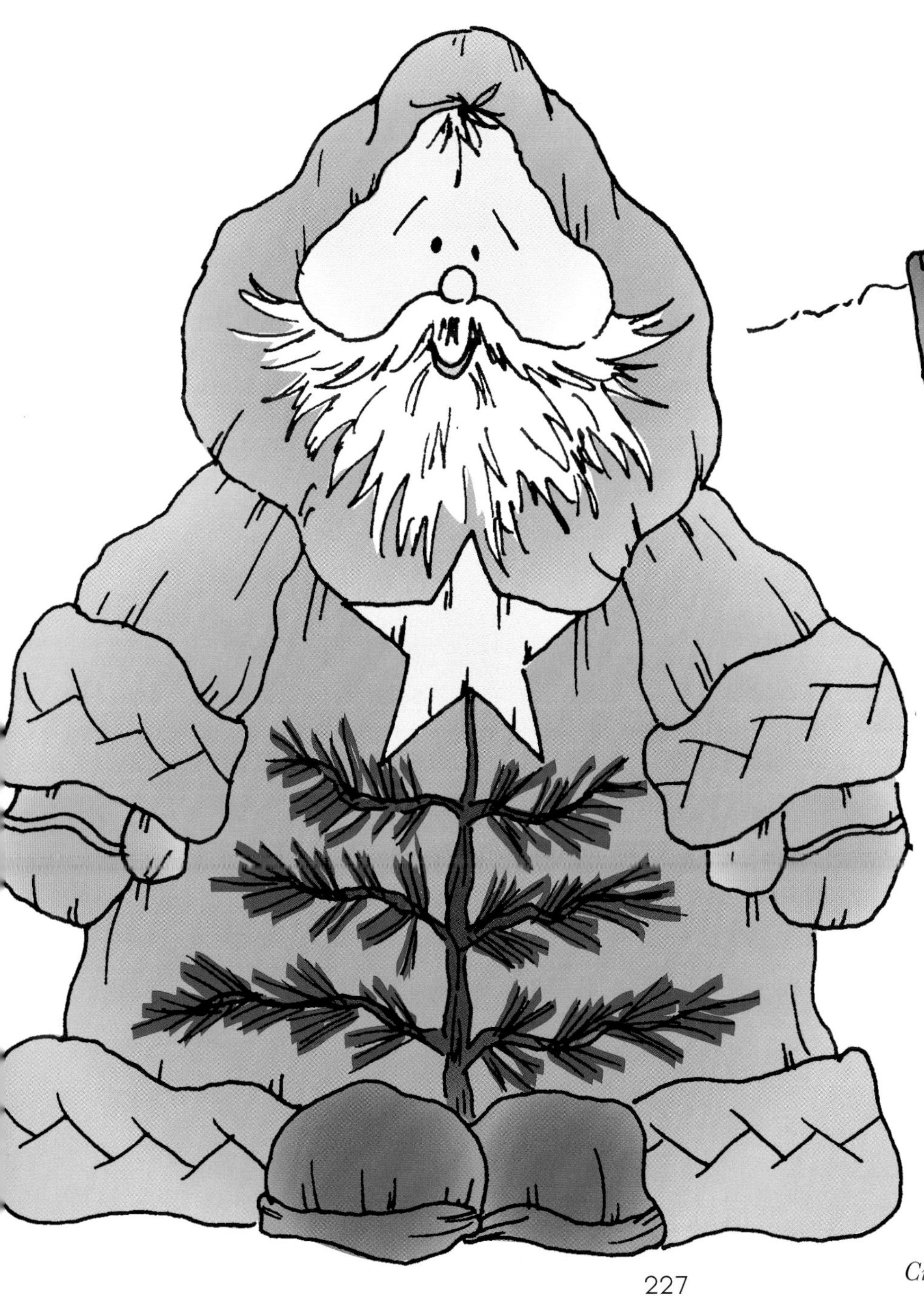

Cindy Mann

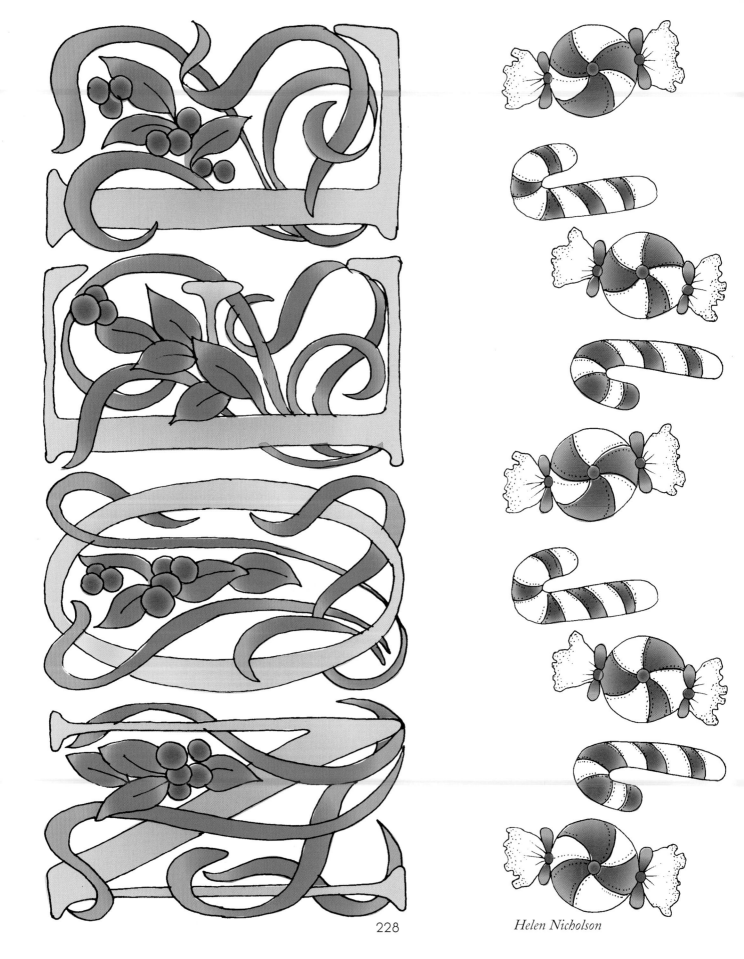

228

Helen Nicholson

Cindy Mann

Gigi Smith-Burns

Cindy Mann

232

Helen Nicholson

233

Cindy Mann

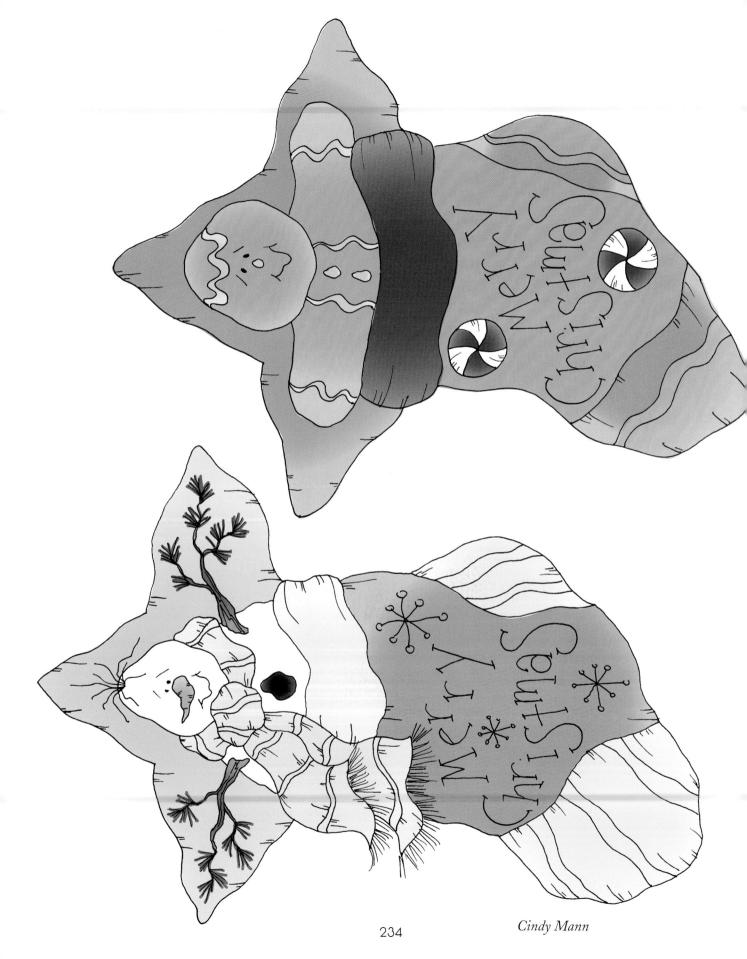

234   *Cindy Mann*

235

Helen Nicholson

236

Karen Embry

237

Cindy Mann

Karen Embry

Cindy Mann

239

Karen Embry

241

Helen Nicholson

242

Susan Fouts-Kline

Susan Fouts-Kline

MISCELLANEOUS

Patty Cox

247

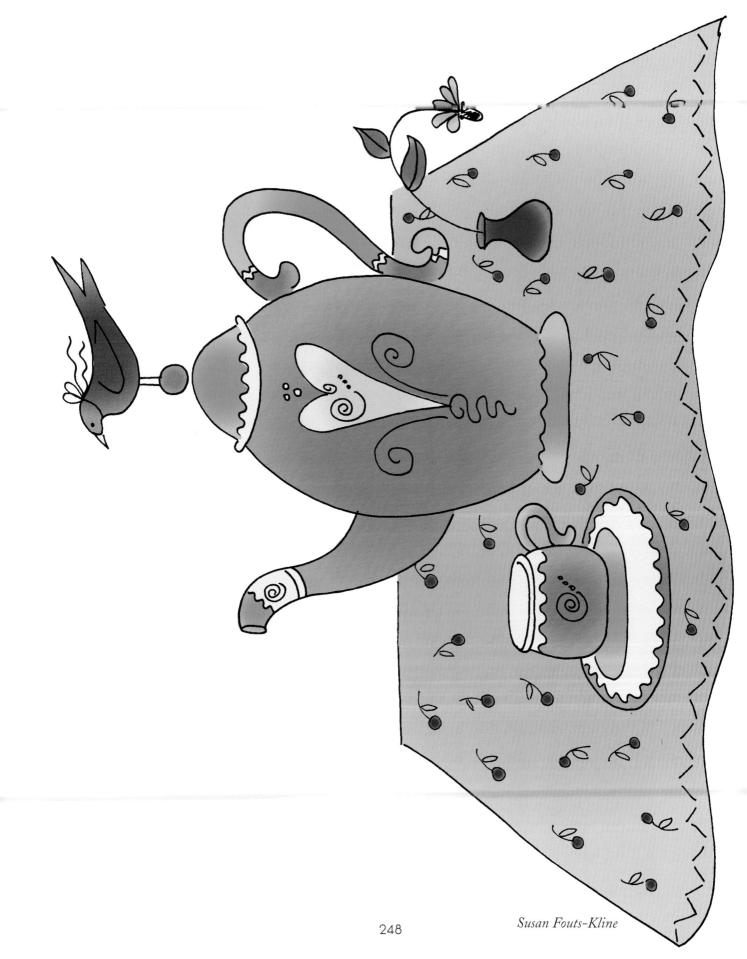

248

Susan Fouts-Kline

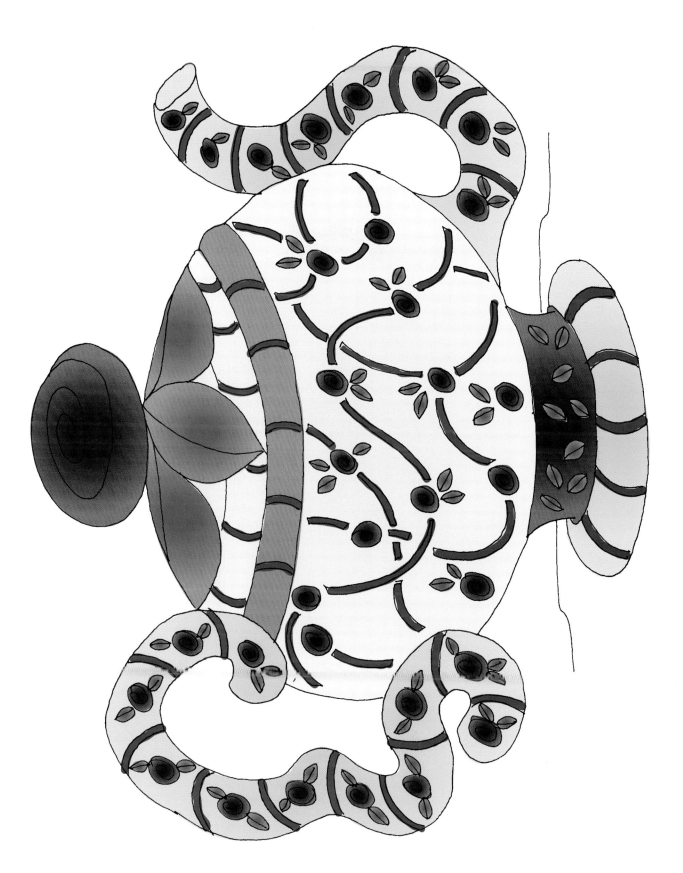

249

Karen Embry

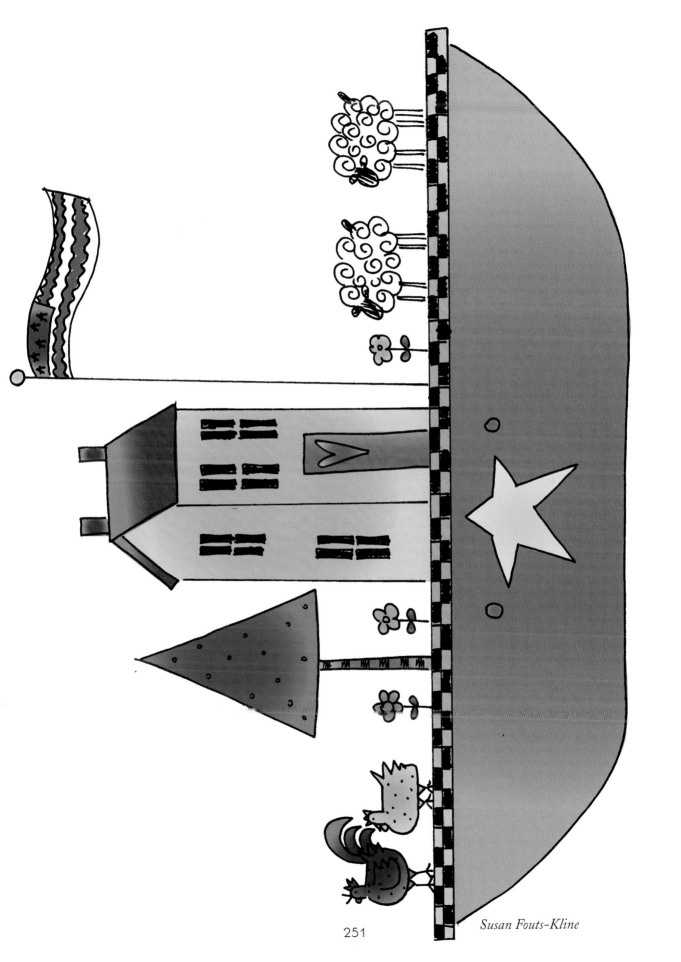

251

Susan Fouts-Kline

Karen Embry

253   *Betty Auth*

QUEEN FOR A DAY

254

Karen Embry

Karen Embry

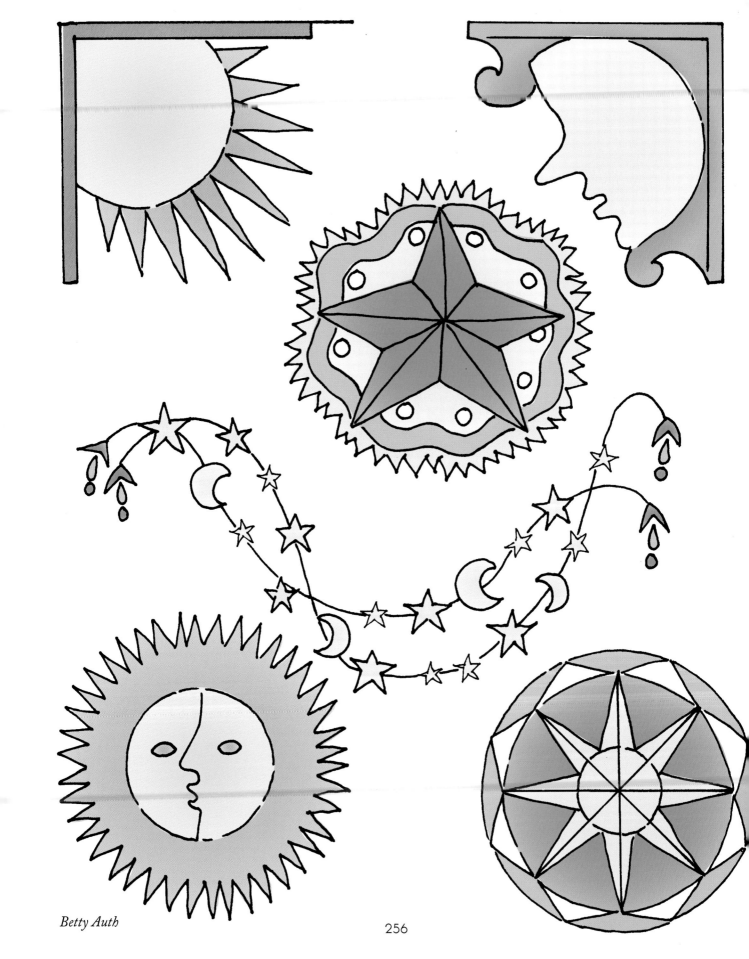